Awaken The Christ Within You

Alexander Soltys Jones

Awaken The Christ Within You

Address inquires to the author:

Alexander Soltys Jones
PO Box 188
Millbrook, Ontario L0A 1G0
Canada
www.alexmeditation.com

Published by:
Cygnet Publications
Cygnet Media Group Inc.
www.cygnetmediagroup.com

ISBN: 978-1-63020-039-8

Dedication

To Jesus, who became the Christ
and inspires us to do the same

Table of Contents

Acknowledgments

From the depths of my soul I would like to thank Jesus Christ for the intuitions he has given me and for inspiring and guiding me in the writing of *Awaken the Christ Within You*. I would like to thank Paramahansa Yogananda, whose writings and teachings form the bedrock of my spiritual life and are the foundation of many of the concepts in this book. I would also like to acknowledge Saint Teresa of Avila, Saint John of the Cross, the authors of the Gnostic Gospels and many other saints, whose words of truth grace the following pages.

With deepest gratitude and appreciation I thank George Johnston for his invaluable assistance in editing and for offering priceless suggestions and content. George, your profound knowledge of spiritual principles and your precision for detail have made this book what it is. Teresa Spanjer, thank you for your friendship, commitment, and your initial editing of this book and its message.

Maureen McDonald, thank you for reviewing the manuscript and for your valuable suggestions.

"Ye are gods;
and all of you
are children of the Most High"
Psalms 82:6

"Ye are gods"
John 10:34

Introduction

Ye are Gods!

By the authority invested in me by the Heavenly Father and our Lord and Savior, Jesus Christ, and the Holy Spirit I testify you are a soul made in the image of God. You are a Christ.

Jesus expressed this truth in a different way and claimed that you are a God. When the Pharisees accused Jesus of blasphemy for saying, "I and my Father are one," he reminded the Pharisees of what their scriptures proclaimed, you are gods and all of you are children of the Most High.

When I was studying for my Bachelors of Religious Education I asked many professors and other Christians the meaning of Jesus words, "Ye are gods." The answer I was given was that Jesus was trying to bewilder the Pharisees. No. Jesus was offering them the good news and essence of his teaching. He was affirming to the Pharisees, and also to you and me, that we are not only a human being but also a god, just like him.

Jesus never focused on how great he was or asked for people's praise. He was more concerned with revealing the divinity in all souls. Outward expressions of praise for God and adoring Jesus' personality help us to become focused on God and Jesus, but are only beginning steps in the inner journey to salvation. Expanding our consciousness to receive our Christ—or God-like—essence is what really counts. Jesus encourages us and says, "What I have done you can do also. What I am you too can become."

As outlined in the following pages, by living in the light of Jesus and by practicing what he taught, you will be able to attune yourself with his state of "Christ Consciousness." Through direct personal and prayerful inner communion of your soul with Christ and as a result of his guidance and help, you will realize the truth that he uttered for all of humankind: "*Ye are gods.*"

In order to experience the truth of Jesus' declaration that "Ye are gods" we must first realize that we are a Christ. The purpose of this book is to help you to focus on and claim your Christ-like nature by unfolding the potential for this state of consciousness that is already within you. The easiest way to attain the "Christ" state of consciousness is to inwardly attune ourselves with Jesus and become one with the state of consciousness he attained.

1

The Christ Essence

The immortal part of your consciousness is your perfect soul, your Christ-like essence. Philip tells us in his Gnostic Gospel that "a horse brings forth a horse, and a man begets a man, but God brings forth a god."

Not only did Jesus but also you and I have the potential to become a Christ. In Christian Theology "Christ" is defined as one person who is perfectly human and perfectly divine but this doctrine omits the truth that perfect divinity is in the soul of every person and simply needs to be discovered and expressed. Jesus realized that he was a Son of God–the Christ–and so can we.

The day God created you in His [think "Her" if you prefer] divine, perfect image you were saved. Or more correctly you have been saved for eternity since your soul, being a part of God, is immortal. You are the soul and are endowed already with eternal life. All that is required of you is to bring this awareness to your remembrance.

Illustration of Becoming a Christ

There was a devout man who heard about an old monk in a Christian monastery who was very saintly. He went to see him and they talked about various things. He asked the monk if he had any regrets, or if he had made any mistakes during his life in the monastery. Upon reflection the old monk replied, "They call me a Christian, but I have not become a Christ."

The man was speechless, as he had never heard of Christ Consciousness, that everyone is eligible to become a Christ. All his life he only thought in terms of the physical person of Jesus Christ. "Is it possible to become a Christ?" he wondered. The old monk continued: "I had put a distance between Christ and myself. In my reading, in my searching and in my prayers I realized that all these years I was deploring the distance and did not realize that it was I myself who was creating it. I now know there is no distance."

A major obstacle in the search for God and Christ is that we create distance. We do not accept the fact that Christ is omnipresent and therefore within us all the time. In our thoughts and actions we push Him away, thinking He is not near. One of the greatest helps on the spiritual path then is to cultivate the feeling that God and Christ are closer than we can possibly imagine. Then we will begin to realize in our attunement and oneness with them that we also are omnipresent.

A great secret of progress in your personal evolution is to consider, not only that Christ is within you, but that in potential you are a Christ. In the essence of your soul you are an immortal child of God. As an immortal soul wedded to a flesh and blood human form, you are a Christ in the making, just as Jesus was, although you may not be presently aware of your Christ-like potential.

Christ Consciousness is a universal state of consciousness latent within you as a Son or Daughter of God made in God's image. Although this omnipresent, blissful state of consciousness is within you, it needs to unfold and be brought to your remembrance.

To become a Christ is to fully realize you already are an immortal child of God and possess *all the attributes of God.* This is exactly what Jesus accomplished as He uplifted His consciousness to become a Christ.

As a Christ you are infinite, eternal, omniscient, omnipresent, and totally free. You are cosmic light, unconditional love, and flawless peace. You possess all-knowing, pure intuition, and as the soul above all forms of suffering in body, mind and spirit, you are ecstatic joy, or ever new bliss.

All these divine blessings are yours as a Christ. Just as Jesus realized he had all these qualities within himself and manifested them in his life, *so can you and I.*

Meister Eckhart, the Christian mystic, clearly expresses in his sermon 18 that in essence not only is Jesus the "Only Begotten Son," but *everyone* has the same potential: "In eternity, the Father begets the Son in his own likeness…The Father ceaselessly begets his Son and, what is more, he begets me as his Son–the self-same Son! Indeed, I assert that he begets me not only as his Son but as Himself and Himself as myself, begetting me in his own nature, His own being… My physical father is not my real Father… He may be dead and yet I am alive. Therefore, the Heavenly Father is my true Father and I am his Son and have all that I have from him. I am identically his Son and no other, because the Father does only one kind of thing, making no distinctions. Thus it is that *I am his only begotten Son.*"

Along with Meister Eckhart we too can claim we are "a Christ."

2

The Gnostic Scriptures Reveal the Christ

At the beginning of the Christian era there existed a collection of Gnostic gospels that were circulated and used by Christians. Many of these devout Christians were interested in having more than a faith relationship with Truth, or God, and wrote and used these scriptures as a guide to help them to experience Christ within themselves. Some of these gospels were discovered in the Egyptian Desert at Nag Hammadi in 1945.

The discovery of the Gnostic Gospels offers us an insight into what some of the early Christians believed and practiced before the Church shaped Christianity according to its design. Unfortunately orthodox Christians in the middle of the second century denounced these sacred scriptures as heresy.

Not all of the Gnostic texts are reliable as many border on the fantastic, and it is therefore understandable why the Church denounced them, but unfortunately in disregarding all of them many texts that shed light on Jesus' true teachings were considered heresy.

The valid Gnostic scriptures ("Gnostic" means bestowing knowledge) also offer traditions about Jesus and reveal intimate conversations between Jesus and His disciples. The Gospel of Mary sheds new light on Jesus' relationship with Mary Magdalene. The Gospel of Thomas and the Gospel of Philip reveal esoteric, mystical knowledge that is not found in the New Testament.

In these sacred texts Jesus speaks to his disciples of the world being an illusion and of how to attain enlightenment, rather than of humankind being in sin and in need of repentance. Jesus is thus portrayed as a spiritual guide who opens access to spiritual understanding rather than, as traditional, orthodox Christianity sees him, as being Lord and the Son of God in a unique way, different in essence from the rest of humanity whom he came to save.

From the Gnostic Gospels we encounter Jesus as a messenger of knowledge who helps to uplift his followers to have an intuitive experience or insight of the ultimate reality through the process of knowing oneself. According to Jesus, to know oneself at the deepest level is equivalent to knowing oneself as a Christ. In union, or oneness, with God one realizes the truth, "Ye are gods."

In the Gospel of Thomas, perhaps the best known of the Gnostic scriptures, Jesus tells Thomas he "drinks" from the same intoxicating, bubbling stream of consciousness that he has shared with others and that he is therefore no longer his master. "I am no longer your master because you have drunk and have become intoxicated from the bubbling stream that I have measured out." In another verse from the Gospel of Thomas, Jesus clearly emphasizes this same truth: "He who will drink from my mouth [imbibe the same wisdom I possess] will become just like me. I myself shall become he, and the things that are hidden will be revealed to him."

In our time, just as with Thomas, Jesus is assuring us that we can know and become one with his state of consciousness and, through this union, realize the Christ within us.

In the Gnostic scriptures, the Gospel of Philip emphasizes the difference between the names "Jesus" and "Christ." Philip appears to be telling us that "Jesus" is a name that hides and "Christ" is a name that reveals. "Jesus" identifies the master in terms of a specific lifetime, while "Christ" refers to his universal, omnipresent consciousness. Philip says, "For this reason 'Jesus' is not particular to any language; rather he is always called by the name 'Jesus.'" Philip also says that the Christ or Messiah is *universal* and others have this name according to their own language. He goes on to say that "Christ [universal, omnipresent, all-encompassing consciousness, or Christ Consciousness] has everything in himself, whether man, or angel, or mystery, and the Father." Philip says Jesus is exalted because he revealed the Christ in his own life.

In Buddhism this universal state of consciousness is called the Buddha Nature and in the Hindu scriptures is called Krishna Consciousness. These names refer to the all-encompassing, universal state of consciousness that Jesus attained.

Jesus, Buddha and Krishna manifested their Christ-like essence, their divine nature, both inwardly by their refined states of consciousness and as a result outwardly in their life-transforming actions. In this book we will look at both the interior consciousness and the resulting outer expression, focusing predominately on the life of Jesus.

3

Christ State Manifested Outwardly

In a lecture, Daya Mata of Self-Realization Fellowship told everyone in the audience that they craved power. She then asked why we crave power so much. The answer she gave is that we already know in some deeper level of our being that we are all-powerful. As children of God we intuitively know we are nothing less than one with Infinite Power.

God has placed a yearning within us, where we can never be content until we realize our *all-powerful Christ nature*. Unfortunately this craving for power becomes distorted when a person does not realize the infinite power they seek is already a part of their Christ-like nature and tries to find and express it in the world. In seeking power a person may try to control others. They may strive to rise to the top of the corporate ladder in an endeavor to feel all-powerful.

In some cases this quest for ultimate power goes to the extreme, where one tries to conquer the world, for example the conquests of Alexander the Great, Hitler and many others down through the ages.

Jesus connected with the infinite power within himself and manifested his all-powerful nature. He was able to bring about so much good in the world. With his dynamic power of love he was able to move and uplift hearts, helping others to discover their own Christ nature.

The Gospels reveal so many different ways in which Jesus was able to manifest his omnipotence. He used his power to calm others and bring them to God, to heal people, to control nature–calming a raging sea–and had the power to change water into wine.

One of the greatest examples of Jesus manifesting his supreme power and perfect self-control was during his crucifixion. He had the power to call upon twelve legions of angels to destroy his adversaries if he desired. He could have used God's infinite cosmic energy and with one glance he could have destroyed those who were crucifying Him.

Instead of using his power in these limiting ways, Jesus did absolutely nothing. He held on to his calm and with perfect self-control and humility gave himself as a willing sacrifice and went through the crucifixion. Later on we will look at the various lessons and benefits Jesus' crucifixion gave to the world. What Jesus did reveals his Christ essence.

In the same way Mahatma Gandhi manifested his power when an assassin shot him, and his final gesture was not one of violence or aggression but was a humble gesture of forgiveness. Gandhi put his hands together and nodded his head, offering a blessing of forgiveness to the one who was taking his (mortal) life away.

Through the divine soul power that flowed through him because of his selfless love and dedication to truth, non-violence, and high ideals, Gandhi was able to bring about India's freedom from one of the greatest military powers in the world.

Reflect on the truth that divine power is within you, waiting to be expressed, just as it was by Jesus and Gandhi, through the perfect channel of pure and loving intention, humility, and dedication to truth and God.

Our Separation from Our Christ-like Essence

Dr. Elizabeth-Kubler Ross was a Swiss woman who worked with the terminally ill. She assisted them by counseling and encouraging them, but also took the time to observe and study them. She records her findings in her books.

Here is a remarkable observation she offered. She said you would think, because the strongest instinct is self-preservation, not only in humankind but animals and plants, that the greatest fear would be the fear of death. From her observations of thousands of terminally ill patients she said there is something worse, much worse: "The feeling at the end of life that I have not really lived."

People come into this world with the feeling they want to accomplish something important, not realizing it is to manifest their Christ-like essence and remember that they "are gods" and therefore act like a god in their life. At the end of life they feel they have come up short and their life was spent in vain. Many who have had successful careers, some being so popular in the eyes of the world they became household names, having all the money and fame they could dream of, still feel at the end of life they have not accomplished what they really came on earth to do. They sense that they have not really lived, and just do not know what it is they were ultimately looking for.

Elvis Presley said in an interview that he was one of the loneliest people in the world. Richard Chamberlain gave a very profound recollection of his life when he said that he was laughing on the outside but crying on the inside. Freddie Mercury, the lead singer of the British rock group Queen, wrote in one of his last songs on the Miracle album: "Does anybody know what we are living for?" He had amassed a huge fortune and had attracted thousands of fans but this did not satisfy him. In an interview just before his death he admitted he was desperately lonely. He said, "You can have everything in the world and still be the loneliest man, and that is the most-bitter type of loneliness. Success has brought me world idolization and millions of pounds, but it prevented me from having the one thing we all need–a loving, ongoing relationship."

What we are all looking for is a relationship with God and direct personal communion with God until, in blissful union with God, we realize our Christ essence, our God-like nature.

Leo Tolstoy, author of *War and Peace*, wrote a book called *A Confession* about his search for meaning and purpose in life. First he tried to get as much pleasure out of life by drinking heavily, gambling, living promiscuously, and leading a wild life. This did not satisfy him. He then desired to acquire money. He inherited an estate and made a large amount of money from his books, yet this did not satisfy him either. Next he focused on a desire for fame, importance and success. He tells how the Encyclopedia Britannica describes his book as "one of the two or three greatest novels in world literature." Even the achievement of this success left him unsatisfied. He then became ambitious for a family and to provide them with the best life could offer. He got married to a kind, loving wife and had thirteen children and found this distracted him from any real search for the purpose and meaning of life.

Leo Tolstoy had acquired the best life could offer and yet he admits one question brought him to the verge of suicide: "Is there any meaning in my life which will not be annihilated by the inevitability of death awaiting me?" In his observation of life he saw people were not asking the basic questions of life: "Where did I come from? Who am I, and where am I heading? What is life about?" Eventually Leo Tolstoy became a devout Christian.

Most people get caught up in a busy life with a career and many other things, but at the end of life they feel that something is missing. Fortunately, we do not have to wait for the end of life because God gives us a warning about halfway through. It is called the mid-life crisis. It is very real and most people experience it.

In a mid-life crisis people begin to question their life. They begin to realize they have been extremely busy building a career, having a family and many other pursuits. But something is missing; they are not really satisfied. People then panic as they look ahead and think about what they are going to do with the rest of their life. They question what will happen if they continue in the same direction. Overwhelmed with fear, they may go to extremes and do really bizarre and crazy things hoping to catch some type of meaning or purpose in their life. Instead of looking within, they may look for some outward solution.

Perhaps a man will leave his wife and run away with a young woman. Or a person may travel or move away to another country, completely changing his or her lifestyle in an effort to grasp onto something, thinking, "This is it, the answer to my emptiness." A woman who has been busy all her life working and building a career may stop and question herself. She might think, "I have lost track of time and the years have slipped by; my biological clock is ticking away and I am not married." She may begin to think that she wants to have a child, that this is the missing element in her life.

In the mid-life crisis, real panic sets in and people tend to focus on external solutions. An external solution is not the solution because we are the soul. We are immortal children of God. We are a Christ and it is only in realization of our infinite Christ nature that we can be fully satisfied.

We can be truly ourselves only when we understand that we are made in the image of God and have access to the divine attributes of God within us, and then begin to feel and express these divine qualities.

God and the Christ within you are waiting with infinite patience for you to be redeemed. And deep within, you yearn to know exactly who and what you are. You are not just a physical being but are a child of God, and you will never be satisfied until you experience the peace, love and bliss of the soul.

So many people feel they have a mission to fulfill, and they are right, but they misinterpret the divine mission that has been given to everyone as an external mission. Although an external mission is important, it should never eclipse our mission to realize God. Some may say that God gives their outer mission to them and this may be true, but our mission to realize God's presence within us as the Christ is an ongoing mission and lasts until we become liberated.

Jesus was a supreme example of becoming a Christ (*Christed*). If we would walk in the footsteps of Jesus and follow his example we will manifest the Christ within us.

4

The Purpose of Life is to Know God

Jesus knew he was the Christ and one with God and declared that the kingdom of God is at hand and we all can know we are a Christ and one with God. When we model Jesus he will lead us to our oneness with God. Union with Spirit is our ultimate responsibility and God-given destiny. Jesus wants us to know this truth through experience and Self-realization not mere belief. Belief is just the first step. Belief in God sustains us until we actually experience our oneness with the Divine.

You know that you crave fulfillment, a feeling of completeness and satisfaction. You desperately yearn for a happiness that is constant and does not depend on a world of change. You desire a love that is unconditional. In essence you are seeking God. You not only yearn for a fulfilling and satisfying relationship with your Creator, but the deeper, refined part of your consciousness will never be content until you become *united* with your Source once again.

I can testify by my own life and the lives of many I have ministered to that there will always be a deep feeling of incompleteness and emptiness until the void within you is saturated with the presence of God. Nothing—*nothing*—outside of you can ever fill this inner void.

No matter what fantasy you may be entertaining in your mind and heart, even if you fulfill it you will still not be satisfied or fully happy. Regardless of how convinced you are that this or that will make you happy, you will ultimately find it does not.

Of course, it is extremely important that you fulfill your outer responsibilities and be practical in your dealings with the world. But no matter how hard you try to appease the feeling of emptiness and loneliness with external possessions and experiences you will always end up feeling dissatisfied. Only God can complete you. God is the one necessity in your life you cannot do without. Many have tried to get along without God, but I guarantee if you try this approach to life you will end up frustrated and discontent.

Unfortunately, it usually takes a long time—only after much suffering and disappointment—before an individual comes to realize it is a relationship with and *experience* of God they really want. It only takes a little reflection and observation of the state of the world around us to perceive this is true. Who can truly claim they are content and fulfilled? Even those who are working intensely for God in the world will find themselves still empty and incomplete if their consciousness is only external. *It is only those who deeply commune with and are centered in God who can speak of total satisfaction and contentment.* In their relationship with God they gradually realize their oneness with God.

I would like to direct and encourage you to focus on the only solution to your underlying problem of unhappiness and dissatisfaction. Until you are seeking God earnestly there is always some longing deep inside that drives you down first one path and then another seeking that ever-elusive state—perfect happiness. The "something else" that you are seeking is God.

The French philosopher Blaise Pascal says that everyone has "a God-shaped hole" in describing the spiritual vacuum people feel and the sense that they are in exile. Every human heart yearns to fill this hole with the presence of God and feel complete and at rest once again. St. Augustine expressed this longing very well when he said, "You have made us for yourself, O Lord, and our heart is restless until it rests in you." Everyone is a child of God and therefore hard-wired for God.

It is God and God alone who can take away the underlying pain in your heart and sense of loneliness and incompleteness, because God's nature is unconditional love, peace and joy. The love of God throbs just behind the beat of your heart and flows through all forms of love … for family, friends, and beloved.

Above all God loves you unconditionally—without any reservations—and God's perfect love for you is greater than any human heart can possibly equal and give. No person or thing can satisfy your heart–only God can.

Those who have not found God are suffering with a broken heart. It cannot be otherwise, for only the love of God can complete and mend our hearts. Our hearts have been broken many times thinking that in this or that relationship we will find the perfect love we crave. There is only one love that is perfect: God's love.

Remember, the unconditional love of God is *within you*, so it can be experienced at any time you make yourself receptive to receive God's grace. Receiving God's grace is receiving your divine birthright as an immortal son or daughter of God: your ultimate Christ-like nature and your oneness with God.

God is infinite, and includes all divine attributes within Him. We are a ray or spark of God's infinite love and light, and have God's attributes at the core of our being. God's nature of peace, love and bliss transcends all restlessness, pain and sorrow. Divine bliss is the all-satisfying joy we crave. To be permanently united in God's changeless peace and overcome all traces of sorrow and suffering, and also become fully established in the joy of God is an intuitive experience that transcends mere belief. This is the supreme purpose of not only religion but also life itself.

Infinite Bliss-Consciousness or Rapture

The joy of God I am speaking about, and which Jesus endorses, is beyond any sensory experience or intellectual and emotional elation. It is rightly called in the Bible a *state of rapture*. Christian mystics who have touched the Bliss of God describe it as incomprehensible. It is an experience of total happiness and complete fulfillment. The joy that is attained through God realization is ever new, endless delight and can never grow stale.

The highest experience of God we can have is to feel Eternal Bliss. In Bliss every other aspect of Divinity—for example, love, wisdom, peace, immortality—is fully contained.

Jesus affirms that he attained this state of consciousness and will help uplift your consciousness beyond all suffering until you too are permanently united in the ecstasy of God. Jesus said, "In this world you have tribulation (suffering) but be of good cheer because I have overcome the world."

In John, Jesus tells his disciples, and also encourages us, that when he returns (when we receive him within) our hearts shall rejoice, and our joy no man can take from us. He promises us our sorrow shall be turned into joy, and if we tune in with him our joy will be full.

Saint John of the Cross tells us the first passion of the soul, our Christ essence, is bliss. I remember a Jesuit priest saying that humankind has a low tolerance to bliss. Most people I talk to do not know the full meaning of the word bliss. Indeed we set our standard way too low, thinking that some outer condition will give us the pure joy and happiness we crave. It will never happen that way. Also we fail to realize that the little bit of happiness we feel from the pleasures of the world fails in comparison to the pure joy of God.

In the Old Testament Isaiah tells us what we really want and need, and that we will never rest and be at peace with ourselves until we learn how to permanently remove all sorrow and suffering from our life and attain infinite bliss-consciousness, or the state of rapture promised in the gospels. In a poetic way Isaiah says, "With song and everlasting joy upon their heads, they shall obtain joy and gladness, and sorrow and sighing shall flee away."

Bliss is already within us and does not need to be attained but realized. By removing the static of restless thoughts and emotions we realize the Bliss we are.

Paramanhansa Yogananda, who wrote the spiritual classic *Autobiography of a Yogi,* made a statement that transformed my consciousness. He said, "God is all the love of all the lovers who have ever loved." From this quote it is clear that God is the sum total of all love and God's love is unconditional. We can say the same for peace and joy, or any other attribute of God as well. God is the sum total of all happiness or bliss.

In his oneness with God, what did Jesus experience? He realized and felt he was all the love of all the lovers who have ever loved. Jesus also realized he was the sum total of all joy or bliss as well. Jesus not only experienced this state of awareness inwardly but he expressed it in his dealing with the world.

The good news is that this state of consciousness is within you as well, and being a Christ, you are all the love of all the lovers who have ever loved and the fullness of all happiness and joy. As a child of God your essence is Bliss.

God Beyond Gender

In this book, as I talk about God, I am aware that God is neither masculine nor feminine. Jesus tells us that we need to perceive God as Spirit. When Jesus was talking with the woman at the well he said, "God is a Spirit: and they that worship him must worship him in spirit and in truth." God (Spirit) created both the masculine and the feminine principles as equals, but is beyond both.

Because of the limitations of language, in the Bible the word "he" is used to refer to "Spirit." In other spiritual writings, in order to signify that Spirit (or God) is beyond gender, Spirit is often referred to as "It." However, to avoid using a term that usually refers to inanimate things, I often speak of Spirit as "He" or "She." Spirit often manifests in a way that merits personification, and can also be referred to as "Heavenly Father" or "Divine Mother." As you read this book, if you prefer different terms, please mentally change the gender or personification to suit your preference or belief.

In support of the sacred feminine element, acknowledged by Jesus in some of the Gnostic Gospels, I often speak of God as "Mother" unless quoting a New Testament passage or Gnostic scripture where "Father" is specifically used. The Gnostic writings that were used and cherished by first and second-century Christians (before they were denounced as heresy by the orthodox Christian church) often speak of God as Mother, whereas the Bible only speaks of God as Heavenly Father. In his gospel, Philip said, "When we become Christians we have both a Heavenly Father and Divine Mother." In the Gospel of Hebrews, Jesus is quoted as referring to the Holy Ghost as "my mother." "Even so did my mother, the Holy Spirit, take me by one of my hairs, and carry me to the great Mount Tabor."

In my book *Conversations with Christ* I discuss the Trinity, although words and human concepts can only hint at the nature and transcendent glory of God. The **Father** is the Supreme Blissful Intelligence beyond Creation. The **Son,** the "Only Begotten Son" (or Christ Consciousness), is the Father's love and intelligence within Creation. It guides the **Holy Ghost**, the divine Light that creates the universe ("Let there be light and there was light," as mentioned in Genesis).

The Holy Ghost is also spoken of as the Cosmic Sound that emanates from the White Light. It has a vibratory quality, which is heard and felt by many saints and deeply meditating devotees. It is sometimes referred to as the music of the spheres and in Christianity has many names: Holy Ghost (or Holy Spirit), Amen, the Word, the Comforter, the Sound of Many Waters and the Trumpet. This holy, vibratory sound is heard by different people in different ways, and in Hindu scriptures is designated by the syllable OM (or AUM).

The universal Christ Consciousness (the Only Begotten Son) is a state of consciousness and is also beyond gender. Sometimes I call this universal state of consciousness the Only Begotten Daughter of God. When we become one with this state of consciousness we become awakened Sons or Daughters of God.

5

The Christ Within

The ultimate happiness and fulfillment you are seeking is within you as an inner experience of your soul and God. It is a state of consciousness, a state of unity with the consciousness of God. In the Bible this heavenly awareness or consciousness has been called by many different names: the Garden of Eden, Zion, and New Jerusalem. In the scriptures some of these names, although they may be actual physical locations, have often been used to represent intuitive and refined states of perception within oneself.

Throughout the Bible, Jesus and John the Baptist continually proclaimed the good news that the kingdom of God was at hand and is available right here and now. Jesus was very specific and tells us the *kingdom of God is not of this world and is within you.* The kingdom of God reigns in the depths of your heart.

True repentance then is to look within to the soul instead of to worldly things, by developing the soul's all-knowing power of intuition, which alone is aware of truth.

Jesus is sometimes referred to as the kingdom of God because he received the Christ, or universal state of consciousness, in his own consciousness. The omniscient intelligence of God is omnipresent in creation as the Christ Consciousness and is present in every atom of creation.

The Christ Consciousness is not a man with a white beard wearing a robe but is a state of awareness. When Jesus used the pronoun "I" when speaking of this omnipresent state of consciousness, he was referring to the vast, infinite Self of all beings, not to his little human body or personality as Jesus.

The Christ Consciousness encompasses the entire created cosmos. A person who can withdraw their awareness and consciousness from identification with and attachment to the ego and body and unite it with the Infinite, Omnipresent Consciousness can with authority say with Jesus, "I am a Christ." A person who has expanded their awareness to that exalted, omnipresent state can also claim, "I and my Father are one" just as Jesus did. The Father, Son (Christ Consciousness) and the Holy Spirit are not separate gods but are three basic aspects of God as the One (the One Spirit). Each aspect, or "person," contains the other two, so in our union with God as the Christ Consciousness, we also are one with the Father and the Holy Spirit.

When a person becomes one with Spirit his awareness or sense of "I" is no longer limited by the human body. The soul like a wave has merged back into the vast ocean from which it came. The awakened soul becomes the ocean of God.

In the Gospel of John, "Word" refers to the creative, vibratory power of the Holy Ghost guided by the Christ Consciousness. In John's profound declaration at the beginning of his gospel, "In the beginning was the Word, and the Word was with God, and the Word was God" (John 1:1), "Word" is a translation of the Greek word "Logos" used by John. By "Logos" John meant the divine principle or universal, loving intelligence active in Creation. This is what theologians and philosophers in John's time meant by "Logos." In John's account of the beginning of Creation, "Logos" refers to the Cosmic Intelligence, or Christ Consciousness, which guides the Holy Spirit as it creates and sustains the Universe. Later on, mainly due to the work of the theologian Irenaeus, the Logos (Word) in John 1:1-5 and 9-15 was taken to refer only to the person of Jesus as an individual, instead of, as John intended, the loving intelligence of God active throughout Creation, which, as indicated in 1:15-17, manifested Its wisdom, power and glory through Jesus. Because of official Church doctrine established in the early centuries of the Church almost all Christians believe that these verses only pertain to Jesus, and do not realize John was writing of the loving intelligence of the Father manifesting in the cosmos as life and light in the creative power of the Holy Spirit. John calls the Logos

19

the Only Begotten of the Father (the only emanation or reflection of the Father in Creation).

Although the Logos has no gender, the term is a masculine noun in the Greek language, which may have been one of the reasons English translators of the original Greek New Testament used the pronouns "him" and "he" instead of "It" in translating verses that refer to the Logos, for example, "In him was life; and the life was the light of men." These translations undoubtedly have helped to solidify the Christian belief that, in verses 1:1-5 and 9-15 of his gospel, John was speaking only of Jesus.

The idea that Jesus is God as the second "person" of the Holy Trinity–begotten by the Father before the world was made, and coequal with the Father in a way that no other being ever has been or ever will be–has caused sectarian conflict down through the ages. This doctrine has made it appear that Jesus is the exclusive Son of God. However, contemplating verses 1:1-5 and 9-14 in John's Gospel, substituting "It" and "Its" for "he," "him" and "his," will make it evident that "Only Begotten Son," or "Logos," refers to the intelligence, light, and love of God, omnipresent in the universe, manifested in Jesus and other fully enlightened beings, and waiting to be awakened in every one of us. Careful study of the writings of those who have experienced the Logos, which John calls the Only Begotten Son of God, should convince anyone that It is omnipresent, impersonal and universal.

The Book of Proverbs is referring to the Christ Consciousness (or Only Begotten Son of God) when it speaks of God's wisdom (intelligence) in creation. The author personifies wisdom as the first act of creation: "Yahweh created me [Wisdom] when his purpose first unfolded, before the oldest of his works. From everlasting I was firmly set, from the beginning, before earth came into being. ... when he laid the foundations of the earth, I was at his side, a master craftsman, delighting him day after day, ever at play in his presence, at play everywhere in the world, delighting to be with the sons of men" (Proverbs 8:22-23, 30-31; The Jerusalem Bible).

Saint John of the Cross confirms the impersonal nature of the Son in the *Ascent of Mount Carmel*. He writes that the Son of God is wisdom (intelligence) and light. "...when the soul has completely purified and voided itself of all forms and images that can be apprehended, it will remain in this pure and simple light....transformed into simple and pure Wisdom, which is the Son of God."

Jan Van Ruysbroeck, the Flemish mystic, confirms this same truth and tells us in his book *The Adornment of the Spiritual Marriage* that the Light emanating from darkness (God beyond creation or vibration) is the Son of God: "For in this darkness there shines and is born an incomprehensible Light, which is the Son of God, in whom we behold eternal life..."

Jesus is referred to as the Only Son of God because he became one with the Only Begotten Son of God state of consciousness which is another term used to signify the Christ Consciousness. They both represent the omnipresent aspect of the one God–the loving intelligence (Light and Wisdom) of God in every particle of creation–with which the consciousness of Jesus was identified.

Jesus' state of consciousness as the Christ Consciousness is the Only Begotten Son, which Jesus received from God. Jesus did the inner work to become a Christ and Jesus promised through John, "As many as received him (the Christ Consciousness he attained) to them gave he power to be sons of God" just as he was.

God so loved the world He created through His light that He sent forth His intelligence as the Only Begotten Son to guide all living beings back home to their eternal blessedness in God.

Jesus became a Christ by becoming one with the omniscient intelligence of God in all creation. If we experience the full measure of God's wisdom, or intelligence, in creation we too become a Christ. The supreme intelligence of God is already within us; we just need to remember, as Jesus did.

The new creation (new heaven and new earth) will arrive when all humanity (past and present) experiences the same state of consciousness Jesus attained. Jesus reminded the people of his day, and continues to do so, that the kingdom of God is at hand and invites all to go within and receive the kingdom of God by uniting their consciousness with his. Since Jesus has already attained the Christ Consciousness, or Only Begotten Son state of consciousness, through his expanded consciousness he can help us uplift our consciousness, so we can reside in the new heaven and earth (divine consciousness) with him.

Saint John of the Cross tells us in his *Spiritual Canticle* that God's presence and essence reside in the innermost being of the soul. A person who wants to find God should leave behind all things (the senses and the world) and enter within him/herself in deepest reflection and during this time consider all other things as nonexistent. Saint John then quotes Saint Augustine who said, "I did not find You without, O Lord, because I wrongly sought You without, who was within." Isaiah also invites you to enter into your secret chambers, shut the door behind you (close the door of your senses) and hide yourself a little, even for a moment, in God. By going within, you will truly discover your all-satisfying, pristine Christ essence and the true happiness you have been seeking.

The purpose of the Bible then is to help you attain these states of consciousness and dwell in this inner heavenly abode while on earth. Remember, however, to keep this quote of Padre Pio in mind when you study various spiritual writings including the Bible: "Through the study of books one seeks God; by meditation one finds Him."

Your Creator has implanted a yearning within you, coaxing you to seek and attain your refined state of being. Most people misconstrue this inner yearning as desire for material things and conditions and focus all their time on outer pursuits.

Your soul, being made in the image of God, will never rest until you awaken to your pure Christ essence and allow its radiance to shine forth completely in your life. God and Jesus will continue to work in this world until everyone awakens to their infinite immortality and realizes their oneness with God.

If you want to know and become established in your Christ-like nature it is mandatory that you enter within yourself. The proper form of meditation is the greatest practice to help you to go within and meet yourself as the Christ. For meditation instruction, see my book *Meditation: Where East and West Meet.*

Being Born Again, or the Second Birth

When Jesus emphasized that "You must be born again" and said, "Except a man be born again he cannot see the kingdom of God" and "Except a man be born of water and of the Spirit, he cannot enter into the kingdom of God," he was indicating that this "Second Birth" is an intuitional awakening of the soul where the soul apprehends its own nature as "the Christ." This awakening may come about gradually after many rebirths in the physical body (reincarnation).

The only way to be "born again" is actual communion of the soul with God. Buddhism advocates the awakening of intuitive knowledge through meditation to realize the transcendence of Nirvana. Sufism also focuses on the intuitive, mystical experience of the soul. In the Bible, Psalms endorses stillness to gain the intuitive perception to know God.

A Relationship with God and Christ through Jesus

As already affirmed, one of the easiest ways to have a relationship with God and realize your Christ-like nature is through a relationship with Jesus. Jesus has attained the ultimate state of awareness. By walking in his footsteps and attuning ourselves to his state of consciousness, we too can experience all that Jesus experienced and manifested. Jesus became a Son of God. If we become one with him we will also become a Son or Daughter of God. Jesus is one with God and when we become one with Jesus we automatically become one with God.

Knowing God through Jesus is the underlying theme of the New Testament. This is why Jesus said, "I am the way, the truth, and the life: no man cometh unto the Father, but by me." Jesus is telling us the only way we can know our Christ-like stature and the Father is through the Christ Consciousness state that he attained. Jesus is not telling us in this quote that his personality or his body is the only way but that the state of consciousness he attained is the only way. It is by working with him and attuning our consciousness with his that he can help us attain the same state of Christ Consciousness he attained.

Jesus also came to show the intimacy of God and how to approach Him as Father. Jesus knew God as Spirit, "I Am That I Am," but also knew God in the aspect of the Heavenly Father and according to the Gnostic Gospels as Divine Mother.

In our desire to attain Self-realization though developing an inner communion of our soul with God as Spirit, or even as the Heavenly Father/Mother, these concepts may seem a bit too abstract, distant or remote. I have found it may be difficult in the beginning for most people to meditate on God and that establishing a relationship with God through Jesus can be more personal and comforting. A Buddhist may find a deeper relationship with God through Buddha. Buddha also attained the Christ Consciousness state and can uplift his disciples to that state of awareness and help them ultimately become one with Nirvana. The Christ Consciousness state would be known in Buddhism as the Buddha Nature.

A Hindu may find a deeper relationship with God through Lord Krishna. Krishna became one with the Christ Consciousness state, and this is known in India as the Kutastha Chaitanya state of consciousness.

Since Jesus was fully human when he was on earth we can focus on his human form and personality as portrayed in the New Testament in an attempt to uplift our consciousness. We can also get to know Jesus as he is now in his resurrected being and attune our consciousness with his resurrected, omnipresent consciousness.

When we know Jesus and feel his essence within us, Jesus becomes an essential part of our being, and we will encounter our true Christ essence through him. Jesus tells us he is one with the Father, and in his humility he will transfer everything you offer to him directly to God. Your relationship with God is assured through Jesus.

I have one purpose: to help you bring Jesus' presence into your awareness and assist you to feel the peace and joy of your Christ nature in your life. May I help you discover the ways to make yourself receptive to the presence of Jesus and be in tune with Him. To experience and feel his peaceful and loving presence within and all around you, learn how to open your heart fully to Jesus and receive his unfailing guidance and infinite blessings.

Belief is only the first stage in developing and deepening a relationship with Jesus. I desire to assist you to move beyond mere belief to an actual experience of Jesus. Jesus' second coming is available right here and now: it can be experienced within you.

Oneness with Jesus is possible in this lifetime. When you behold your connection and especially your oneness with Christ, you will experience your oneness with God and indescribable joy will fill your life and you will transcend all suffering in body, mind and soul. It is then that true happiness and contentment will be your ongoing reality, for you will know that you too are a Christ.

6

Jesus as He Is

There are many misconceptions surrounding the life of Jesus. In order to help you develop a deeper relationship with Jesus I would like to address some of these issues and then share with you the Jesus I personally experience.

I have already mentioned there have been recent discoveries of manuscripts that date back to early Christian times, providing a fresh insight into the teachings of Jesus Christ and the foundation of Christianity. Due to a misunderstanding of these fragments some scholars challenge the very authenticity of the Gospels and have actually announced that Jesus did not die on the cross, that he survived his crucifixion. It is claimed he went on to marry Mary Magdalene, who produced a "bloodline," which exists to this day. Some of these claims have also been endorsed in very popular books of fiction without proper insight into the life of Christ.

Other writers and scholars have said Jesus did not exist at all; he is only a myth. Some proclaim that if he did live, many of the events recorded in the Gospels–such as the virgin birth of Jesus, his death on the cross and resurrection–did not actually happen, since they are not recorded in some of these recently found manuscripts. Some claim these events are taken from Egyptian Pagan Spirituality. It has been found that other enlightened prophets experienced these events before the birth of Jesus, and sceptics insist these legends were adapted to the life of Christ. In the Gnostic Scriptures, however, Philip the Apostle mentions Jesus' death on the cross several times in his gospel.

I have felt Jesus many times in my life, and through my intuitive perceptions of his indwelling presence I know the accounts recorded in the gospels are valid and true. It is my testimonial that Jesus lived over 2000 years ago, was born of the Virgin Mary, died on the cross, and was resurrected and ascended into heaven, where today he lives in omnipresent glory.

With regard to the claim that Jesus married Mary Magdalene and had children, it is obvious to anyone who has done any deep *inner* spiritual work that Jesus was celibate. In his spiritual marriage with God he used *all* of his energy to unite with Spirit and to do the Divine Will on earth. By his words and actions he made it abundantly clear that doing God's will and helping humanity return to conscious communion with God was the only intention of his life. In the Gospel of Matthew, Jesus emphasizes this way of life to his disciples: "There be eunuchs who have made themselves eunuchs [by self-control] for the kingdom of heaven's sake. He that is able to receive it, let him receive it."

The Gospel of Philip states "Jesus loved Mary Magdalene more than all the other disciples and used to kiss her often." This passage is sometimes taken out of context to indicate that Jesus had a sexual relationship with Mary. Jesus was simply expressing his affection and spiritual love to Mary as a result of her spiritual devotion to him. He kissed her as an expression of his spiritual gratitude for her undying faith and loyalty to him. In Jesus' time, as in many cultures today, kissing was a sign of affection, not necessarily sexual. It was accepted as a way of expressing friendship with another person, regardless of gender. Phillip was not indicating in his Gospel that Jesus and Mary had a sexual relationship. In fact he supported the ascetic way of life and the renunciation of sexual activity.

It is not only my testimony that validates the life and events of Jesus' life. The experiences of many others down through the ages–St Francis of Assisi, St Teresa of Avila, St John of the Cross, St Ignatius, St Anthony, Therese Neumann, to name only a few—indicate that they also accepted the evidence of the Gospels. Saint Francis received the stigmata, or sacred wounds of Jesus, as a testimonial to his oneness with Christ and the truth of his passion. Jesus also appeared to St Francis and conversed with him every night in the forest in a flesh-and-blood form. There have been countless others who claimed they too had direct experience of Jesus and visions of the events of his life on earth.

In the year 338, while the Christian Church was in debate as to the divinity of Jesus, St Anthony came out of the desert and entered the town of Alexandria and proceeded to the church where the debate was being held. He stood up and all he said was, "I have seen him" and walked out of the church. Saint Anthony was so respected as a living saint that the debate ended right then and there. I can also add, "I have felt his presence and heard his voice."

God and Christ as Unconditional Love

Unfortunately, many of the passages in the Bible have been misinterpreted. I wish to offer another interpretation in an effort to help you develop a deeper relationship with God, Christ and truth. Many of these interpretations are not only from my own personal experience but are supported by the Gnostic Gospels and Christian mystics.

The first obstacle so many people face in trying to form a deep and lasting relationship with Jesus is that they have been taught to fear him. It is said, when Jesus came the first time he came in weakness, but when he returns he will come with power and great glory and judge the world. Many, therefore, think of Christ as one who blesses only those who are good and is angry with—perhaps even hates—those who sin. They believe that he will return to earth and personally judge and condemn them.

Everyone has made mistakes, and most people, even if they believe in Jesus and accept him as their personal savior, feel guilty. They find it difficult to forgive themselves and others, and feel they are deserving of punishment. They think Jesus will disown them and judge them with an eternity in Hell or eternal death. Even people who live in love sometimes suffer from this belief and don't realize the truth in Jesus' words, "To those who love much, much is forgiven."

Jesus is pure, unconditional love. How can one possibly fear love and believe Jesus will inflict us with eternal punishment? With eyes of love, Jesus beholds the Christ in you. He sees the perfection—the image of God—in you. He loves you no matter how many mistakes you have made because he is aware of your pure soul essence. Although many have covered their diamond essence with mud and cannot see the divinity within them, he sees it and is constantly trying to help them overcome limiting thoughts and actions so that they too can see it.

Whenever I hear the concept that we are sinners and as sinners we are totally corrupt I recoil. Jesus never said that anyone was a sinner at the core of his or her being. He forgave sins and helped people remove the mud (wrong thoughts or actions, and their consequences) they had placed on their diamond essence, and he always realized that as diamond souls they were "gods."

The more you feel Jesus' presence of love the greater will be your trust in him, and you will find it easy to surrender to his unfailing guidance and support. Jesus' only concern is that you love God more deeply and become united with God.

Julian of Norwich, after having many visions of God, said, "God cannot be angry. God is love. God is wisdom. God is compassion." Anger is a perversion found in humankind; this trait can never be ascribed to God. Anger cannot exist in a state of unconditional peace and love, and this is what God and Christ are.

God is infinite power and has created and maintains the entire cosmos with billions of galaxies. With such power if God could be angry with you or humanity, for one moment, He could wipe you and everyone else out of existence. Even though you have probably made plenty of mistakes, you are still here on planet earth, so it is obvious God is not angry with you.

The Old Testament talks of God as being angry, so the true meaning of these statements needs to be explained. When the prophets in the Old Testament speak of God's anger it is in reference to a law God created, not to God personally. This universal law states that we reap what we sow, or what we put out comes back to us. God established this law in the universe to create balance and harmony.

God does not reward or punish anyone. We create our own destiny through our thoughts and actions, which, as a result of this just law, create consequences that impact our life. The laws of God are always rooted in wisdom.

When the Israelites followed the laws of God, there was prosperity, abundance and a sense of well-being amongst the Jewish nation. If there was conflict with other nations, they easily prevailed because they were in harmony with God's laws and reaped the resulting benefits. God did not *favor* the Jews; He was not *angry* with the other nation. God loves all equally. The Jewish people were simply reaping the benefits of living in harmony with God's laws.

When the Bible says God was angry at the enemy of the Jews it does not mean a personal feeling ascribed to God but it means that this nation was not in harmony with God's laws, which would bring destruction upon them. Similarly, when the Jewish nation was defeated it was not because God was angry with them and inflicted punishment upon them. They were out of harmony with God's laws and reaped the inevitable consequences. This is why whenever the Jewish nation was in trouble the prophets would warn them to repent and live according to the commandments, especially the Ten Commandments.

God respects and honors the law that He has created. He has given everyone free will and independence and will not impose upon this freedom. God would like to help His children and free them from their self-imposed suffering, but will not try to sway our free will by influencing us, or arbitrarily bend His law. After all, the only way many of us learn not to perform wrong actions is by suffering their painful consequences. And unless our love for God is freely given it is not love at all. How else could we be said to truly love God except that we learned through our free-will choices to love Him more than all the charms of the world? God does not demand that we love Him but waits patiently to see if we come to that decision of our own free will.

The law of love is superior to the law of karma (we reap what we sow). If we call upon the mercy and compassion of Divine Mother or Jesus with a pure and sincere heart and if we are ready to be freed from the consequences of our wrong actions, they will transcend the law of karma with their grace.

God is love and eternal joy. If you have a concept of a punishing God I invite you to replace it with a God of supreme love and tender understanding, a God who loves you and is ever trying to uplift and purify you no matter what mistakes you have made.

The Gnostic Gospel of Truth bestows comfort and reassurance by telling us: "The Father is sweet and in His will is what is good." Another passage states, "The children of the Father are His fragrance for they are from the grace of His countenance."

A saint once said: "There is no creature who can realize how much, how sweetly and how tenderly God loves you." Remember God loves you more than you can possibly imagine.

With confidence and assurance seek God and Christ within yourself. St Paul made it very clear that you are the temple of God. Saint John of the Cross tells us that you yourself are the dwelling place and secret chamber of the Eternal Beloved. He says this should be of immense gladness for you in seeing that all your good and hope (everything you have ever wanted) is so close to you as to be within you, or better still, that you cannot be without your God and Savior. He goes on to say it brings special happiness when a person finally realizes God is never absent, not even from a soul who is engulfed in mistakes, let alone those who have done the inner work and are in a state of grace.

The Will of Jesus is permeated with wisdom and is ever seeking our highest evolvement in God. He has assured us his love will be with us always, even unto the end of the world, helping us reclaim our Christ-like nature and union with God.

Jesus' Relationship with Women

From the New Testament it is clear that Jesus and, therefore, his twelve apostles and Paul respected women. Jesus had female as well as male disciples. A unique feature of his ministry is that he honored women and they had important positions in his work.

From scriptural accounts, Jesus' women followers appeared more devoted to Jesus and steadfast in their faith. At the cross it was women who stood beside him along with John; everyone else deserted him. Women were the first to discover the empty tomb. Mary Magdalene was the first to see the risen Christ. Martha and Mary were great followers of Jesus. A woman named Mary anointed Jesus' feet with oil and dried his feet with her hair. Jesus declared that she would be honored due to her devotion to him. In the upper room at Pentecost women disciples were present, and we can imagine that they helped those disciples who were fearful to hold fast in their faith.

Jesus stood apart from other males in his society and protected the woman caught in adultery.

As a result of Jesus' ministry, women were attracted to Christianity and outnumbered men in the early church. Women converted in larger numbers than men. Early Christianity validated women as spiritual equals of men. Unfortunately, Christianity did not claim social equality for women which I know Jesus would have endorsed.

As mentioned Mary Magdalene was the first to behold Jesus in his resurrection. She wept at Jesus' tomb when she saw that he was not there, and rejoiced when she realized he was resurrected. Incidentally, according to Therese Neumann, the Catholic stigmatic, in her visions she saw Jesus first appearing to his mother, Mary, then to Mary Magdalene. I intuitively agree with this, that Jesus would have come to his mother first. However, due to Mary Magdalene's devotion and Jesus' spiritual love for her, she was the first to behold Jesus at the Tomb.

Jesus' Perfect Balance and the Significance of the Terms "Male" and "Female"

Jesus knew himself as a perfect soul, a divine being. From the last section, it is very clear that Jesus saw men and women as spiritual equals. Everyone to him was a manifestation of God.

It is extremely important to understand Jesus' view of women when looking at the terms "male" and "female" and their significance in a spiritual context, especially in the Gospel of Thomas, as we shall see later.

When Jesus and his disciples used the terms "male" and "female" it was not only a reference to the physical body, but they also used these terms in a spiritually symbolic way to refer to a perfected human.

In the New Testament, Jesus made a distinction between his body, "Son of man," and his state of consciousness as the Christ Consciousness, "Son of God." However, in the Gospel of Thomas, Jesus used the word "male" as a spiritual term to mean "pure wisdom," and "female" to mean "pure devotion."

It is vital to understand this distinction. When I was in seminary, a professor laughed and dismissed the whole Gospel of Thomas as heresy because Thomas quoted Jesus as stating that he would "lead Mary [Magdalene] and make her a male" just like him and the disciples and also "every woman who will make herself male will enter the kingdom of God." In these passages, Jesus is not indicating that a male is superior to a female.

31

Jesus and his disciples honored women and viewed males and females as equals, so, by "male," Jesus was not referring to physical attributes but to a quality of the soul. A person would naturally view Jesus' statement as sexist if they did not understanding the deeper, spiritual significance of these terms that Jesus was offering and only associated the term "male" with the human body.

Why did Jesus choose the term "male" for wisdom and "female" for devotion? Jesus knew that, although women and men are equal, in order to be in harmony with the dualistic nature of the physical world, God created men with a greater inclination to reason and women with feeling predominant. The purpose of marriage was to help balance these qualities, a man bringing out his feeling side under the influence of a woman, and a woman manifesting her reasoning ability through association with a man.

Jesus knew a liberated soul manifests a perfect balance of pure feeling (devotion) and pure reason (wisdom). Jesus offered the deeper spiritual significance of the terms "male" and "female" as he had perfected these soul qualities in his own life, and he inspired his disciples to do the same. Jesus was an exemplar of pure wisdom and love from the beginning of his ministry as he had already perfected and liberated himself. However somewhere, sometime in the past (see chapter on reincarnation) Jesus did the necessary spiritual work and became the perfect "spiritual male," transforming reason into pure wisdom. He also became the perfect "spiritual female" by transforming his emotional nature into pure devotion or love.

Jesus is a pure manifestation of unconditional love. His infinite compassion is balanced with flawless wisdom. As we read different accounts of Jesus' life, we admire and revere his expression of tender mercy, the compassionate side of his nature. We are moved and enthralled by his expression of unfathomable wisdom.

Jesus wanted his disciples to achieve this perfect balance, as indicated in the Gospel of Thomas when he said, "When the male is not a male and the female is not a female [by bringing forth and uniting both the male and the female attributes of one's soul] and they become one and the same, then and only then [when you accomplish this in your own consciousness] will you enter the kingdom of God." Jesus clearly indicated in the Gospel of Thomas that the kingdom of God is attained not by having certain physical characteristics, but by transmuting one's reason and feeling into pure wisdom and love and blending the two.

Jesus knew that Mary Magdalene, his beloved disciple, had already developed the feeling aspect of her nature and had perfected it and expressed single-pointed spiritual devotion to him.

Jesus emphasized balancing "male" and "female" because, in ignorance, Simon Peter had suggested Mary should leave them, for in his opinion, "women are not worthy of eternal life." Perhaps Peter was jealous of Mary. Because of her single-pointed devotion, Jesus embraced her as one of his favorite disciples. In order to correct Peter and perhaps to soften his feelings of jealousy and satisfy his heart, Jesus said he would "lead Mary and make her a male" just like him and the disciples. Jesus thus indicated he would awaken and perfect her wisdom (the soul quality she needed to bring out) and balance it with her pure devotion. This is why Jesus said Mary Magdalene would "become a living spirit resembling males, for every woman who will make herself male will enter the kingdom of God." Jesus simply meant that Mary would achieve liberation when she brought out the wisdom (male) side of her nature to complement her (female) side of pure devotion. The beauty of this passage is that Jesus protected Mary and promised to help her perfect herself and gain liberation in Spirit.

It should be noted that Jesus could have also said under different circumstances, and perhaps even counseled Peter, that every male who will make himself female (develop devotion, or the pure, feeling side of his nature) will enter into the kingdom of God, which Peter eventually did.

Intuition, the gift of spiritual knowing, is the nature of the soul and becomes fully manifested when pure wisdom is combined with pure love and compassion. Jesus emphasized that, to enter the kingdom of God, we need to awaken these qualities within ourselves. He knew this because this is exactly what he himself had done. He accomplished the perfect balance of these qualities and, with them, brought forth the pure intuition of his soul. By pure wisdom and pure love he was always in tune with Truth and God. Naturally, it will take time, perhaps lifetimes, for us to perfectly balance the two sides of our nature and attain this far-reaching transformation, but through meditation we may possibly achieve this balance in this life.

7

Reincarnation

Reincarnation is the law of evolution, "being born again," where we keep coming back on earth until we realize our diamond essence once again.

I distinctly remember living in a past life, when I was a monastic and priest in a very strict Catholic order. In my past life I believed in Jesus and invited him into my heart. I dedicated my life to serving him through the church. While I was a priest I followed my vows and under holy obedience I was faithful to the teachings of the church. I taught the Christian doctrine of the time although my heart was troubled by certain beliefs the church forced onto its members. I was in inner rebellion over the killing of so many innocent and holy people under the name of Christianity.

Since I have a recollection of this past life and now in this life I see I have a new body and a new relationship with Jesus, most of my former beliefs based on church doctrine have been altered.

It is clear to me that when I died in my former life as a priest I did not go to Heaven, or if I did, I did not stay there. Nor am I in Hell or lying in Limbo in a grave. I am back on planet earth working on my evolution back to God with Jesus' help and assistance. In my new understanding and realization I know reincarnation is an undisputable fact in my life. I am not only aware of my former life as a priest but others as well.

Reincarnation means that we keep coming back to the physical universe until we have worked out all our earthly desires and realize that we need God more than His gifts and therefore learn to love God with all our heart, soul, mind and strength. In this complete love we can truly love others as ourselves. In this pure state of love we can recognize that not only we but everyone else is a Christ, a "god."

When we finally realize that we are a Christ, an incarnation of God, we are no longer under compulsion to return to earth's shores or any other sphere in the vast Creation of God unless He sends us back to redeem others.

Reincarnation Declared in the Bible

Allow me the opportunity to show you that the law of reincarnation is acknowledged in the Bible.

Jesus very clearly told his disciples that John the Baptist was the reincarnation of Elijah. The Old Testament prophets predicted Elijah's return, as did the Angel Gabriel to Zacharias.

After Moses and Elijah appeared to Jesus and some of the disciples on the Mount of Transfiguration, the disciples asked Jesus, "Why then say the scribes that Elias [Elias is the New Testament, or Greek, translation for "Elijah"] must first come?" And Jesus answered, "Elias truly shall first come, and restore all things. But I say unto you, that Elias is come already, and they knew him not, but have done unto him whatsoever they liked. Likewise shall also the Son of man suffer of them." Then the disciples understood that he spoke to them of John the Baptist (Matthew 17:9-13).

The prophets of the Old Testament also predicted Elijah's reincarnation and that he would be Jesus Christ's precursor. At the end of the Old Testament we read: "Behold I will send you Elijah the prophet before the coming of the great and dreadful day of the Lord" (Malachi 4:5).

The Angel Gabriel told Zacharias that Elisabeth his wife would bear him a son and he would be the reincarnation of Elias (Elijah). Zacharias was instructed to call the baby "John." Gabriel then said, "And many of the children of Israel shall he turn to the Lord their God. And he shall go before him in the spirit and power of Elias, to turn the hearts of the fathers to the children, and the disobedient to the wisdom of the just; to make ready a people prepared for the Lord" (Luke 1:16-17).

In the story of Jesus healing the man who was blind from birth, the disciples ask Jesus if the man himself could have committed the sin that led to his blindness or was it caused by the sin of his parents. Since the man was blind from birth the disciples are obviously asking their Lord if the blindness was from a sin committed by the man in a past life. Jesus says nothing to dispel or correct his disciples' presupposition; rather than dwelling on the origin of the sin, Jesus was more interested in making manifest the works of God. From the disciples' question we can see they not only believed in reincarnation but also that a soul will carry a sin from a previous life into their next life if it is not corrected.

The following passage proves that reincarnation was common knowledge and accepted in Jesus' time. Jesus asked His disciples, "Who do men say that I the Son of man am?" And they said, "Some say that Thou art John the Baptist; some, Elijah; and others, Jeremiah, or one of the prophets" (Matthew 16:13-20). The Jewish people would have never speculated that Jesus was Elijah, Jeremiah or another prophet unless they believed in reincarnation.

Many early Christians accepted reincarnation; the Gnostics and some church fathers embraced it. However, in AD 553, an essential part of the doctrine of reincarnation, namely that the soul exists prior to conception, was declared a heresy by the Second Council of Constantinople.

In the Gnostic Secret Book of John he says that the spirit of life (truth) and the false spirit (falsehood) are competing for the souls of women and men. If the spirit of life increases in a person, when they die they will enter into the eternal rest of God. If a person dies with the false spirit predominant in their consciousness they will be sent back to earth in another body. The round of reincarnation will continue until the soul at last becomes awakened through intuitive Self-knowledge of its divine Christ nature.

Reincarnation allows ample opportunity for a person to overcome their faults, and realize their immortality and Christ-like nature once again. It also allows individuals time to fulfill all their desires, and perfect their talents so they may eventually offer them in selfless service to God.

I realize from my experience of reincarnation that not only I but also everyone else will keep coming back to earth (or another place suited to our needs in God's many mansions) to accomplish whatever God wishes us to do, and to perform the necessary inner work, with the help of Jesus or another divine being, in order to become emancipated just as Jesus was. It is then and only then, when we become awakened by uniting our soul with Spirit, that we will be entitled to stay in Heaven on a permanent basis or perhaps return to earth at God's behest to help others realize the union of their soul with Spirit and hence emancipation. Reincarnation of liberated or nearly liberated saints for a divine mission is implicit in God's declaration to Jeremiah: "Before I formed thee in the belly I knew thee; and before thou camest forth out of the womb I sanctified thee, and I ordained thee a prophet unto the nations" (Jeremiah 1:5).

In Revelations, Jesus promises us: "To him that overcometh will I grant to sit with me in my throne, even as I also overcame, and am set down with my Father in his Throne." When we have done the necessary work and overcome all limiting desires and have worked out all our karma we are totally free.

8

Jesus' Second Coming

In our evolution back to our Christ nature through Jesus' guidance and support, it may also be helpful to understand Jesus' return and the so-called end time. Since I have reincarnated into this new life I can see the world is still here and Jesus' permanent return has not happened, even though I believed in my former lifetime that it could have happened then.

The permanent return of Jesus was the hope of the early Christians; the apostles and the elders were comforting their flocks by telling them that Jesus' return would happen soon and not to worry. In the first statement in Revelations John states that these things will shortly come to pass. There was such a sense of urgency amongst the early Christians that the Eternal kingdom would be here soon that Paul was inspired to counsel followers not to overly concern themselves with things of this world such as marriage and other worldly preoccupations.

There are those in every generation who claim the end time will happen in their lifetime and Jesus will appear in the clouds to rule the earth. There are many today who tell us we are in the final days and the world disasters and end time will happen shortly and Jesus will come in judgment and rule the world. If we do experience disasters it is due to global selfishness and humankind's misuse of the earth.

The true meaning of Jesus' return, or his Second Coming, is an inner revelation. Jesus was very clear when he spoke of the kingdom of God and said it was *not* of this world. He even told us how we may find the Eternal kingdom and his presence when, on many occasions, he proclaimed the good news and declared, "The kingdom of God is within you."

We do not need to invite Jesus into our life; he is already there within us. Being one with Christ Consciousness he is omnipresent–within everyone. All we need to do is awaken to his indwelling presence of unconditional love and joy. What a comfort to know Jesus is within each and every heart, whether they are a believer nor not. When we do believe in him and then make the *effort* to open our heart and receive him, becoming aware of his indwelling presence, then our life changes and we are truly born again. It is then that we truly know that we too are a Christ.

Jesus is always tender and unconditionally loving in his relationship with you. And he is approachable; his presence is always available for you. He is ever compassionate and endowed with infinite wisdom, offering unlimited guidance and support. Jesus' nature is also pure Bliss—a joy beyond anything this world can possibly offer. To behold Jesus in this special way is an inner experience available to anyone who prepares him/herself to be receptive to receive his sublime presence. Many who have had an inner experience of Jesus testify to his merciful and loving presence.

A misconception most people have been taught is that Jesus' return will be in a physical body. Through misunderstanding of Jesus' words, the clergy often claim Jesus will appear in a physical form on the clouds sometime in the future and will judge all people and accept a chosen few into heaven; the rest of God's children will be banished to a place of eternal punishment due to their sins. People have been conditioned to dwell on a physical return of Jesus instead of experiencing him within themselves. Concentration on receiving Christ in their life is then only perceived as a preparation to being with him sometime in the *future* instead of being totally united with him *now* and receiving his *inner* kingdom.

Jesus has been crucified once, but his teachings have been crucified many times, hindering his followers from preparing themselves to be united with him. The return Jesus spoke about is an inner experience available to all of God's children, no matter what their nationality or color.

In Jesus' Olivet prophecy he predicted the destruction of the temple of Jerusalem and some of the many misfortunes destined to plague the world. At the very end he especially emphasized his return and was very specific that some of the people of his generation would experience his second coming. Indeed Jesus' disciples experienced him in his resurrection, but, more important, his disciples and many others experienced him as the indwelling loving Lord.

In every generation there have been those who have revealed their uplifting experience of Jesus within themselves. Saint Paul speaks about his experience of the resurrected Jesus as "Christ in Me."

The misconception of a return of Jesus in a physical body to rule all nations and usher in the kingdom of God on earth comes from a misunderstanding of Jesus' mission on earth. The Jewish people were waiting for a Messiah to come and free them from their bondage to the Romans. Throughout the history of the Jewish nation anyone who freed the Jews from bondage was considered to be a Messiah, the Christ, or Son of God. Everyone was expecting this of Jesus, even his disciples. They continued to express this hope when Jesus reappeared to them in his resurrection. The Jewish sentiment was very strong for an external deliverance from the Romans. The hope was Jesus would accomplish this during his lifetime and if he did not he would come back as the supernatural Lord and conquer all nations and establish his kingdom on earth.

Jesus never claimed he would return in a physical body to rule all nations. Jesus' kingdom is the kingdom of God, and it is attained when the soul returns to the Father—reunites with God. Jesus wanted people to look within themselves and find this kingdom within, just as he had done. Jesus wants us to realize that we too are a Christ made in God's image.

The kingdom of God Jesus continually referred to is within and around everyone. In the Gnostic Gospel of Thomas, Jesus' disciples asked, "When will the kingdom come?" Jesus answered, "It will not come by waiting for it. People will not say, 'Look! It is here or behold it over there!' The kingdom of The Heavenly Father is spread out upon the earth and people do not see it." The gospel of Luke confirms Jesus' affirmation that the kingdom of God is within, "The kingdom of God cometh not with observation: Neither shall they say, Lo here! or, lo there! for, behold, the kingdom of God is within you"(Luke 17:20-21).

The kingdom of God is a dimension of such a refined, delicate vibration that an individual needs to still themselves of their normally restless mind to perceive this subtle realm. Jesus' vibration is also so refined that, in order to feel it, one usually has to calm their normally restless mind and heart of fear, anger, low self-esteem, jealousy, pride and other forms of agitation.

Again, in the Gospel of Thomas, Jesus' disciples said to him: "When will the kingdom come?" and Jesus replied, "What you are seeking has already come, but you do not realize it." His disciples then asked him when he would reveal himself that they would be able to see him. Obviously Jesus' disciples were looking for a deeper connection to and perception of him than his physical body.

Jesus answered this question as follows: "When you disrobe without being ashamed and place your clothes under your feet like little children and tread on them, then you will see the Son of the Living One and no longer entertain any fear." In other words, separate your consciousness from awareness of the physical body, which the soul is temporarily wearing to enjoy and gain knowledge of the world of matter, and be non-attached to your body. When you rise above sense experiences and intellect, and the idea that they can give you ultimate fulfillment and satisfaction, you will see the "Son of the Living One," the Christ Consciousness, and you will transcend the suffering of the world and "no longer entertain any fear." When the soul is awakened it manifests its infinite nature of courage and strength.

Jesus will come at any time to anyone who is sincerely seeking his help. Many experience his grace and an inner transformation of their lives and accept him as their personal savior. Jesus wants us to go even deeper in our relationship with him, to fully receive his indwelling presence and eternal kingdom. Jesus yearns for us to consciously try to calm our heart and mind to create the necessary stillness to know him as he truly is.

In Jesus' time very few could appreciate the science of stillness and the understanding of experiencing subtle–more refined–vibrations within themselves. To the masses Jesus only spoke in parables, but to his disciples he revealed how they could enter the kingdom of God within themselves.

When Jesus and the authors of the New Testament said he would come with the clouds they were using a term people could relate to, in order to convey an inner experience. Jesus as radiant White Light can be experienced *within* as coming out of the clouds that are separating us from him. In Matthew, Jesus described the inner experience of his presence as lightning shining from the east to the west.

Jesus, as Light, is just behind the darkness of our closed eyes. When, through inner vision, we see the Light of Christ coming from beyond our restless thoughts and desires, we will penetrate the inner darkness and as the Bible tells us, "Every eye shall see Him." Jesus' Love also is hidden–behind the ego's anxious thoughts and fears—and if we would only turn to him within we would feel his indwelling compassion and tender presence.

Jesus, as Spirit, is omniscient and omnipotent. His throne is omnipresence and he is everywhere. He is within all hearts and his presence is within every atom of creation. Since Jesus is omnipresent in the cosmos he would never confine himself to a physical body to rule a material planet forever. It would be far too limiting for Jesus to confine himself in a cramped body for eternity. Asking him to do so, expecting him to forsake his absolute freedom in Spirit, would be selfish on our part. Jesus, however, can and sometimes does materialize and appear in a physical body in order to respond to the devotional call of a sincere devotee.

The true Second Coming of Jesus is to first feel his peaceful, tender, and loving presence within you. In his unconditional love is his undying guidance and support. As you go deeper into Jesus' presence you will experience his joy transporting your soul into ecstasy.

When you become one with Jesus' presence by merging in his loving, blissful, omnipresent, omniscient and omnipotent nature, or consciousness, you too will experience your Christ-like nature free from all limitations. Then you will know you too are a Christ.

The kingdom of God is within you. Remember, all that is necessary is to look within yourself, and you will find him with all his glory and blessings, ever ready to uplift you.

Why postpone your connection with Jesus by trying to know him through mere concepts and beliefs when by experiencing your oneness with him you can know him in Spirit as he truly is.

Since God has given you free will, it is you who have to choose to go within and create the necessary stillness to experience your oneness with Jesus. Jesus is ever waiting for your return in him. Jesus and all the angels are waiting with open arms, and there will be much rejoicing in the subtle Heavenly realms upon your awakening in Christ.

9

The End Time

When will the world end? Many are predicting it will happen in our lifetime, but this is not in harmony with God's cosmic plan.

The purpose of life is to know and love God. This is not just a passing sentiment but is the evolutionary plan of the cosmos. The law of evolution is progression under the direction of the law of love. When a person has learned and is able to unconditionally love the Lord their God with *all* their heart, mind, soul and strength, they will have fulfilled the purpose of their life.

God has created the dream drama of creation from His cosmic thoughts and is drawing all beings back unto Himself through love. When one totally merges one's consciousness in the magnetic, drawing power of love they are automatically drawn back into union with God. When an individual has accomplished this they are then liberated in God and are no longer compelled to return to earth to participate in the cosmic drama of creation. If they do return to earth it is through the request of God, to assist other souls to develop the unconditional love of God necessary to attain their liberation.

When an individual is liberated in love they have reached the end time—the final death mentioned in the scriptures: death of all sorrows, but actually eternal life—where they are no longer forced by desires and the law of karma (we reap what we sow) to return to earth. Jesus promised us in Revelations that we will not have to reincarnate on earth if we do the inner work: "He that overcometh, I will make him a pillar in the temple of my God, and he shall go no more out."

The only reason a soul returns to earth is to reap karmic experiences and fulfill earthly desires. If an individual has merged their consciousness in the love of God and their earthly karma and desires are satisfied, they no longer need to return to earth.

God has given and will continue to give everyone sufficient opportunities to work out their evolution until they come to realize the love of God is the only thing that will satisfy their heart. God is patient and will wait no matter how many mistakes a person makes. He gives each person sufficient time to work out their limiting tendencies and begin their evolution back to Him through love.

When all souls have learned their earthly lessons and the bonds that tie them to this plane have been severed, then the true end-time will have arrived and the times will be fulfilled as promised by Jesus. At that time the planet will no longer be needed to fulfill its duty of being a residence for souls to work out their evolutional progress. Since the earth will no longer be necessary in God's evolutionary plan, God will release its atoms and the earth will cease to exist.

In the Gnostic Gospel of Mary (Mary Magdalene), Mary asks Jesus, "Will all matter be destroyed at the end time?" Jesus responds to Mary's question and reassures her that all nature with its various forms and creatures are interrelated, that they "exist in and with one another" and will return to God "resolved again into their own roots."

The idea that the world will end soon and there will be an official final judgment at some particular time and place is not part of God's plan of love. The Last Judgment talked about in the Bible is not a final judgment. For each soul, it comes at the point of death. It is a time for a review of one's life: "Am I satisfied with my life, with the opportunities to love that I had?"

In this review it is determined whether we have to come back to this school of love to have new opportunities to make good, to learn the lessons we haven't learned yet. This review is the Last Judgment, but it is not a final condemnation. To reincarnate back on earth is the "second death" mentioned in Revelations. "Be thou faithful unto death, and I will give thee a crown of life.... He that overcometh shall not be hurt of the second death."

The concept that a compassionate God of Love would have His children who have died wait in limbo in graves for an undetermined amount of time for a final judgment is also not part of God's loving evolutional plan. A soul whose body has died has vacated it and is drawn back to earth or to another mansion of the Infinite Father. In a new body it will have new opportunities to work on fulfilling its desires and developing unconditional love.

Naturally, each soul is progressing at its own rate of development and it will take time and many experiences before a soul is firmly rooted in the unconditional love of God. The truth is, every soul already loves God unconditionally and yearns for God alone and intuitively knows only God can satisfy it. All that is necessary is to become awakened to this state. When we can accomplish this then our sojourn in dream realms of the Heavenly Father is no longer necessary, as we are free to abide eternally in Spirit.

When souls no longer need to return to this dream earth, it will no longer have a purpose, and the true end time for our planet will have arrived.

The higher purpose of God, to restore the kingdom and the cosmic order, will be achieved when all souls are again in oneness with their source: God.

10

Ye are Gods!

This profound truth, stated in the Introduction to this book, is declared in Psalms 82:6: "I have said: Ye are gods, and all of you are children of the Most High." Genesis tells us: "So God created man in his own image, in the image of God created he him; male and female created he them." Saint Bernard tells us: "In those respects in which the soul is unlike God it is also unlike itself."

Here is a remarkable quote from the discovered manuscripts of the Gospel of Thomas that says it all: "God's kingdom dwells in your heart and all around you. When you know your Self you too shall be known! You will be aware that you are the sons and daughters of our living Father. But if you fail to know your own Self you are in hardship and are that hardship." Until you know your Christ-like nature you will continue to experience many hardships.

As a divine soul you are perfect. Jesus tells us to be perfect as our Father in Heaven is perfect. If we did not have the potential to be perfect Jesus would never have asked us to be so. All that is necessary is to absorb oneself in one's own perfection.

Since God created you as a perfect soul it would be helpful to know what your perfected nature is. Being made in God's perfect image, if you know what God's nature is you will be aware of your own. All scriptures agree God is perfect love, perfect peace, perfect joy, omnipresent, omniscient and omnipotent. All these qualities are your birthright as a child of God. You do not need to acquire them; all you need to do is uncover and rediscover what you already have and that you truly are a Christ.

Here is an illustration that has worked wonders for me and many I have ministered to. As I have explained in another section of this book we can compare ourselves to an exquisitely beautiful diamond that has unfortunately been covered with mud. A diamond is ever pure, ever was and ever will be, no matter how much mud is placed upon it. The same is true of us. We were given the gift of eternal life and endowed with infinite, noble qualities when God created us as an immortal soul. God created us out of His own essence. God established His covenant with us when He created us in His perfect image, and promised and has given us the eternal treasure of His own nature. The only problem is we have, sadly, forgotten our heritage. We need to confidently reclaim the promised land of our divine consciousness and be a light to all nations.

The Gnostic Gospel of Philip uses an example of a pearl that falls into the mud and becomes dirty and stained. He says whether the pearl is covered in mud or has been washed in balsam oil and made clean it is "always precious in the eyes of its owner." In the same way the sons and daughters of God, no matter where they are or what they have done, are still precious in the sight of God.

Jesus can help clean us up so that we may realize we have always been and ever will be the precious diamond or pearl in the sight of God. Jesus said in the Gospel of Philip: "Blessed is he who *is* [the perfect soul, or Self] before he came into being [was immersed in creation]. For he who *is* has been and shall be [as the eternal soul, as a Christ]."

Creation and the Forces of Good and Evil

Who can fathom the motives of God in creating this fabulous universe of whirling galaxies, suns, moons and planets, ours alive with an incredible variety of life forms, and inhabited by people of different races, with different customs? Although our planet is rife with conflict, war and destruction, it was not that way in the beginning, and may once again become an Eden of beauty, harmony and love. In the meantime, we need to reclaim our birthright as divine, immortal beings, created by an infinitely loving Father, who desires that we end the loneliness and suffering we have endured for countless lifetimes and return home.

God is Love and Spirit. As Spirit, God is infinite oneness. In order for God to create this universe, its living beings, and an ever changing drama of events and human experiences, God needed to create diversity in a part of Himself. So He thought of multiplicity and vibrated His consciousness with thoughts of diversity and contrast. First, God thought of every aspect of Creation in His infinite consciousness, then, through His will and His energy, the cosmos was materialized as His Cosmic Body.

Since God is omnipresent, nothing can be outside of Him. He is the Essence of everything that exists, and all things are made out of Him. He created extraordinary beauty and variety in the world to make possible a wide variety of experiences for human beings. But for humans to lose their awareness of oneness–the indivisible unity of all things in Creation–and to perceive sharp contrasts as dualities (opposites) was not God's doing. The possibility that humans would become enmeshed in perceptions of dualities was there, but they could have retained their consciousness of the oneness of all things while also perceiving contrasts.

A passage from Isaiah (45:6-7) confirms the Lord is the Source of everything:

I am the Lord there is no other God beside Me.
I formed the light and create darkness,
I make peace and create evil;
I the Lord do all these things.

Before creation, there was no time, no space, no objects, nothing but God. God was formless, infinite, indivisible Spirit; and Bliss, Love, Power and Potential. But these aspects of God were one. In order to bring about creation, God needed to separate a portion of Himself into many different aspects of Himself. There needed to be contrasts, so out of Himself, God created the Elohim, archangels entrusted with great creative powers, who, in turn, manifested realms of great beauty and magnificence and then created the physical universe. Through God's delegated power, there came forth energies, galaxies, planets, and physical forms. Objects of different colors, sizes and shapes, as well as sounds, tastes and so on were created so that God's soul children (who are aspects of Himself) could interact with Him and each other while living in a physical environment of beauty and variety, with limitless opportunities to extend God's Creation.

Whatever God's motives were in creating the universe and souls–individual expressions of Himself, endowed with their own free will–we can be sure His motives were rooted in love. As a perfect Father and Mother, He would have loved His soul children and wanted to see them interact and enjoy His Creation. This was His supreme plan of goodness. From God's consciousness, or thoughts, of goodness and beauty our physical universe was created. And, for reasons that can only be rooted in God's perfect love for His soul children–each one unique and made of His eternal substance–God put them in bodies to enjoy His Creation and live in harmony and love.

When the Lord says, in the book of Isaiah, that He forms and creates all these things it is important to understand that, before anything is created by Him or His children, He has already created the thought of it as a potential, or possibility, in His consciousness. God has thought of everything that could possibly happen, as a potential, or possibility, and God is responsible for the infinite variety of possible occurrences that could ever emerge in Creation.

God does not manifest, or create, peace and evil in Creation. He has given His children the power to do this. God, in His love, has given His children freedom to choose and manifest anything that He has conceived in His mind.

God's children, however, cannot create thoughts, for they are universally rooted and originated by God. They can only think or do what has already been conceived by God. God's children therefore use God's thoughts by drawing these thoughts to them and then, if they do act upon them, they become responsible for those actions and the consequences.

If a person dwells on God's thoughts of goodness and acts upon these thoughts then the result will be goodness for the world and that individual. The Bible affirms this truth when it says we reap what we sow. If we draw a negative thought to us, dwell on it, and act on it, then there will be negative consequences in our life and hence the world.

Although God has thought of every moral evil and sin as possibilities, and allows them to occur if His Children decide to choose them, God does not create moral evil in the world. God's loving plan is only for goodness and every good and perfect gift for His children. If God's children choose His loving plan then this world becomes an Eden but if they choose the opposite then this world becomes a hades. By choosing the latter, Satan has manifested much of the evil of this present world, and unfortunately, people have brought many evil things upon themselves by their own actions.

Job suffered for reasons only God could fully understand. If we are suffering, we cannot help but wonder why, and we naturally seek an explanation in terms of past wrong actions, the desire to share karma (some saints have suffered to take away the pain of others), or some other reason. But, having done all we can to remedy our plight and discover the reason for it, many of us need to simply surrender to it, knowing that God is a loving God, Creator of the heavens and earth, whose intelligence and power are far beyond our comprehension and whose ways are rooted in love. This was the lesson learned by Job, who, because of his loyalty to God despite his sufferings, grew into a more expanded relationship with and understanding of God.

With regard to suffering and things we cannot explain, we can draw solace from Isaiah 55:8-9, "For my thoughts are not your thoughts, neither are your ways my ways…. For as the heavens are higher than the earth, so are my ways higher than your ways, and my thoughts than your thoughts."

Sometimes suffering is a catalyst to advance us toward seeking union with God, which may not have happened in any other way.

God is a tangible, loving God, who is in our hearts and souls, nearer than the near, but who reveals Himself to those who seek Him earnestly and sincerely, not to those who are spiteful and arrogant, or who seek Him, not for His bliss and love but because they hope He will give them material success and power, or who do not seek Him because they are more interested in earthly pleasures. Of course, God may come to anyone at any time, regardless of what they think or do, but to cultivate a close relationship with God, the following virtues are very important: selfless love and devotion, sincerity, good will to all people regardless of their actions, willingness to know and do God's will, moral behavior, and serious contemplation of the testimony of those who have known God and manifested His presence in their lives.

Knowing that God has created the universe out of love brings comfort and strengthens our faith. God created the highest heavens and other realms, including the physical universe, through the White Light, the first manifesting vibration. When God decreed, "Let there be light and there was light," as mentioned in Genesis, the White Light brought forth into manifestation some of God's ideas. There are two forces in the light: an externalizing (or dividing) force, or energy, of creative power, that manifests Creation and an internalizing (or unifying) force, or energy, of attraction or love, that guides the work of the externalizing force so that all things reflect goodness, harmony, beauty, love, oneness, and divine principles. Both of these forces create by using God's ideas that are in the Light.

Both the externalizing and the internalizing forces are intelligent forces and are archangels of God. The Christ Consciousness we have been speaking of guides the internalizing force in its creative work.

For our physical universe, God imagined contrasting experiences, such as ebb and flow, light and dark, pleasure and pain. As mentioned, He did not create them to be experienced as opposites, or dualities, although He would have known that, with freedom of choice, we might perceive them in that way. In addition to wholesome pleasures and things that were good, He would have envisioned the possibility that extreme pain and evil might occur in the cosmic drama He had set in motion, for He had given His creative, externalizing force and human beings free will. But for them to bring suffering and other evils into existence was not His intention. We can assume that, being omniscient, God had thought of every possible occurrence that might transpire in His playhouse of the universe, but because He had given the actors freedom of choice, did not know what they would choose to do.

God gave the externalizing force, or archangel, the responsibility to create the world so we would enjoy it, and along with individuality and independence, souls were given a thin veil of separation from The Infinite so that they could participate in the cosmic drama without dissolving into total unity with God. If you like you can perceive the action of the externalizing force as similar to the scientific theory of the "Big Bang" explosion of cosmic creation. The externalizing force created space, time, subatomic particles and every other constituent and form in the physical universe out of the divine energy, or light, of God.

After human beings were created, they began to perceive their experiences in terms of likes and dislikes. Because they liked pleasurable experiences and disliked painful ones, they mentally rejected the latter and judged them as bad even though pain was far less intense when their consciousness was united with the bliss of God and served a good purpose by alerting them to harmful influences and things to be avoided. By judging some things as bad or evil, they began to perceive things dualistically, as good or evil, and by mentally rejecting things they didn't like, they were unable to see all things as united in the oneness of Spirit.

Oneness is the nature of God, who, as infinite, omnipresent Spirit, embraces all things as one, so their awareness of God and of the soul, which was created by God in His image and likeness, was diminished. The more their awareness of the all-satisfying bliss and love found in God and the soul was diminished, the more they tried to fill the void by seeking happiness in the physical world. As a result, they became attached to the body and sense pleasures. Many became selfish and denied the love at the core of their being.

In creating beings with freedom of choice, God created the potential for both benign and destructive aspects in the universe. In the cosmic dream of God there is beauty and good, but owing to the wrong choices of many of the beings He created, beauty has often been distorted, and goodness replaced with selfishness, fear and hate.

God's plan was that the two forces, or archangels, would work in harmony. The externalizing (or dividing) force brought into manifestation the idea of change, or time, in the Unchanging and the idea of division, or space, in the Undivided. The externalizing force also brought into manifestation God's idea of particles of Light. We can imagine the externalizing force in the first creative vibration of God (the White Light) creating a vast sea of irreducible particles, or waves, of light in a realm of time and space. All creation is composed of innumerable particles of indivisible spiritual light, which make up the basic subatomic particles that, in turn, make up the much larger units that physicists today call atoms. In ancient times, however, the word "atom" meant the most basic building block of the universe. Atoms were elementary, irreducible particles, from which all physical substances were created. From the point of view of sacred teachings, these, the most elementary constituents of all matter, are particles, or waves, of spiritual light.

The internalizing (or unifying) force, as part of or guided by the Christ Consciousness, shone on the atoms, or particles, of spiritual light and further spiritualized them. Under the influence of the magnetic power of love (in its pure divinity and glory), vast quantities of these basic, adamantine particles of God's light came together in a multitude of ways to form the physical components of the universe.

The spiritualizing force of intelligent Christ Consciousness arranged these particles in such a way as to form the mineral, the plant, and then the animal kingdom. When, through the spiritualizing work of the Christ Consciousness, souls have advanced and have passed through the lower forms to the pinnacle of the animal kingdom, they then take on a human body.

God's original perfect plan of goodness was to use the internalizing and externalizing forces to create only good and beauty in creation as seen in Genesis, "And God saw everything He had made, and, behold, it was very good." When God first created man and woman He created them so that their awareness of their oneness with Spirit—the Changeless, One, Eternal Reality—was only partially veiled. Adam and Eve (who symbolize the first humans to inhabit the earth) were in a divine state of consciousness (Eden) and were aware of their oneness with God and the beauty and goodness of creation.

When God created human beings He endowed them with sacred centers of consciousness and energy in the spine (chakras), which manifested the glory of God. God intended humans to live in rapture, aware of the contrasts in the world so that they might be entertained by the cosmic show, but absorbed in oneness with Him in a non-attached, blissful state of consciousness. Their inner awareness was always turned toward Spirit in the spiritual eye, the single eye referred to by Jesus. After a perfect existence these divine human beings, manifested by God out of God's very being, were to return home in oneness with God.

God's original plan was that after the soul took on a human body, it was to remember its innate ability to procreate by materializing a physical form for an incoming soul and also be able to dematerialize its own body at will at death. God's liberating and generous plan for His children was that, after a perfect existence in a human form, their souls were to merge in the Infinite Spirit easily and painlessly.

This frightened the externalizing force, for he perceived that, if all souls eventually merged in God, then there would be no need for Creation and his work would come to an end (see the chapter: The End Time). The externalizing force knew he would lose his creative power, and would have to eventually go back to God. The externalizing force was not pleased with this idea and became Satan, the fallen archangel. Ever since the creation of the human species he has been creating havoc to divert the awareness of humanity from awareness of God, and by means of his temptations, causing us to focus instead on the world of matter and become identified with our physical body.

God's original plan made it easy for His children to pass from this world into the next, to leave their body and go home to God in complete oneness with Him. Due to Satan's rebellion this process is now very different and much more difficult, with untold suffering and misery.

How the Christ Consciousness manifests in the human mind and body and how Satan influences us is a very complex subject and is beyond the scope of this book. However, we can see that, in the human mind, Christ Consciousness guides the higher intelligence to realize that only God and the soul can satisfy. Christ Consciousness works in harmony with the soul. Satan works through the lower mind, or ego, which is identified with the body and senses.

In our own minds we can perceive a struggle between the influence of Christ Consciousness, which is moving us forward toward awareness of the soul and God, and the influence of Satan, keeping us attached to things of the world. Above all, Satan is intent on keeping us focused on the senses and worldly preoccupations so we will forget our diamond essence and union with God. Satan will do anything to try to prevent us from realizing we are a Christ.

Because this intelligent, externalizing (or dividing) force, or archangel, rebelled and became Satan, we can say it is now working to destroy anything that uplifts humanity and brings us home to the paradise within us. In the oppositional qualities of good and evil, it is working with the negative polarity of evil—greed, jealousy, fear and so on. Satan works to manifest an ugly counterpart for every beautiful creation of God's goodness in body, mind and nature.

We should realize, however, that good and evil are not equal forces, and good was not created to oppose evil. For love—the highest good—is the supreme, ever-existing power of God, while fear, greed and other forms of evil are simply the result of the denial of love. Evil is not a primal force, as is love, and will vanish when all souls are liberated from evil and become enlightened.

Satan, or the serpent, influenced Adam and Eve, and they lost their awareness of oneness with God and became caught up and ensnared in the dualities of creation. By succumbing to his temptations their energy was turned away from God toward matter.

God placed the pristine souls of our progenitors, symbolized by Adam and Eve, in perfect bodies, and these beings had great spiritual powers and awareness. God told them they could eat the fruit (enjoy the sensory experiences) of any of the trees (sensory organs) in the garden (physical body) but not of the tree of the knowledge of good and evil in the midst of the garden (in the middle of the body). And He said that if they did, they would die (lose their divine bliss-consciousness and spiritual power).

The sex organs are located in the middle of the body, and the meaning of the allegory is that God was telling them not to have sex and thereby become engrossed in the physical sensations of the body. Experiencing sex would bring their kundalini energy and consciousness down from their spiritual centers of divine awareness (chakras) in the brain and spine, so that their awareness would be focused primarily on bodily sensations instead of spiritual realities, and they would become engrossed in the world of matter and the consciousness of the lower mind, or ego.

Even though God had warned Adam and Eve not to eat the fruit of the tree of the knowledge of good and evil in the midst of the garden, Satan tricked them into doing this. As a consequence, they lost their exalted state of awareness and had to produce children by the lesser method of sexual propagation, which till then had been limited to animals. Before they fell from the heaven of divine consciousness (Eden) they had the ability to materialize offspring through spiritual intention and will; now they were no longer able to remain in the paradise of Eden and had to endure a life of toil and hardship.

Because of Satan's influence on the original humans and their fall, all of humanity is born with the perception of duality in creation (which is the "knowledge of good and evil" promised by Satan) and have little awareness of their oneness with God. The soul is always one with God but due to Satan's influence this awareness is diminished or forgotten. Perfection is in our soul, in its awareness of the oneness of everything, and our oneness with everything can never be experienced solely by the physical body and mind, which perceive the world in a dualistic and extremely limited way. Satan however tries to convince us that perfect happiness can be found in sense pleasures or the "ideal life."

Satan continues to perpetuate attachment to physical pleasures, material possessions, and worldly ambitions, so we will be unaware of the beauty and bliss of God and keep on reincarnating, drawn back again and again by unsatisfied, earthly desires. He tries to induce thoughts of selfishness, mistrust, jealousy, hate and vengeance in our minds to get us to be inconsiderate of others and to abuse or harm them, creating bad karma and the need to reincarnate. He wants us to be stuck in creation, reincarnating again and again, so there will be no need for him to surrender to the state of oneness with God. If all souls go back to God and there is no more need for a physical plane–which is his domain–then Satan will be out of a job. Satan is intent on keeping his job. He uses the tools of likes and dislikes, our emotional involvement in the oppositional states, to keep us bound, preventing us from seeing the One Reality in all contrasts.

Satan's main tactic is to prevent us from knowing that we are a Christ, a divine child of God. He uses subtle means to convince us that we are unworthy (sinners) and unfit to be called a child of God.

In its most inclusive definition, evil is anything that keeps us from perceiving God's omnipresence, omniscience and other divine qualities and hence our own divinity. Satan manifests evil to delude us and influence us to choose actions that turn us away from God. Good, in contrast, is that which gives us realization of God and our essential unity with God.

Another subtle trick Satan uses is disease and ill health and the pain and suffering that result, to cause us to crave the perfection of good health. When pain is excruciating it increases our desire for appeasement. We come to fear and hate ill health and form a compelling desire for good health, which keeps us bound in the duality of creation. The soul is connected to the body through the crown and other chakras but, as the Higher Self, its essence, the soul is beyond the body and therefore its state of good or ill health.

Of course it was God's plan of goodness that we have perfect health and prosperity while here on earth. After a perfect existence of health and prosperity in a human body, we were to merge in oneness in Spirit by dematerializing our body at will, instead of suffering a painful death.

While on earth we should strive for health and prosperity, as this is our birthright as children of God, but Satan distorts this natural urge and increases our desire and compulsion for perfect health, eternal youth, and a perfect body image.

Satan increases our desire for prosperity and causes us to crave the pleasures of the world and hope for perfect physical fulfillment. He also instills in us the fear of poverty so we get caught up in the oppositional states and the desire to reincarnate to find perfect prosperity here on earth. Ever since the temptation and fall of the first humans, this world has been a battleground between good and evil, and until it once again becomes an Eden, good and evil will ever alternate in supremacy.

Satan strives to increase our desire to see perfect pictures in an imperfect world. The yearning for perfection that we feel can only be fulfilled in the soul and God.

We are already perfect in our Christ State—the diamond essence of our soul—which contains everything. But, unless we are Self-realized (enlightened), we are unaware of the spiritual riches within us and lose sight of the fact that we do not need to acquire anything else. Our ultimate joy and satisfaction is in the Self (the Higher Self), which is beyond the limitations of the body. We can use the body, mind and sense perceptions to enjoy the world, but as long as we are limited by them, we will never feel complete.

As we continue our spiritual work we come to realize that the only lasting and fully satisfying prosperity is the love, bliss and inner fulfillment found by living in harmony with God and by experiencing God within us. Jesus said, "I and my Father are one." When we realize our Christ-like essence, as Jesus did, then we can claim we are one with the Father. Jesus is omnipresent with God and knows the universe as his cosmic body and that he contains all things within his consciousness. Jesus possesses everything and this is true prosperity. Like Jesus our soul is always prosperous, being one with the owner of the universe. God is omnipresent and owns everything, and as children of God, when we realize we are omnipresent with Him, we too realize we own everything. In oneness with the owner of the universe we have everything, as He does.

Moreover, a God-realized master, being one with God, can manifest at will whatever they wish. Satan knew that Jesus could manifest whatever he wanted and tempted him to convert stones into bread in the wilderness. Jesus knew this was not the will of God at this time and chose not to do so. A God-realized master once said he had to be very careful about what he thought and wished for because he would receive it instantly. When God gave Adam and Eve the power to materialize a body and dematerialize it at will, he also gave them the ability to materialize whatever else they needed. As a soul made in the image of God we also have that innate, God-given ability.

God wants us to be prosperous while we are in the world, for this is our true nature as a child of God. This was God's original plan. He wanted us to act as His immortal children on earth expressing all of His divine qualities.

If we are not manifesting prosperity then we need to work for it mentally and physically. As divine children made in the image of God our birthright is to have an equal share of the earth's bounty. If we do not have our equal share we need to demand our birthright from God. As well as demanding our birthright we need to work conscientiously towards prosperity with the attitude of pleasing God. If we work to serve and help others then our actions are pleasing to God and will bring the required prosperity. We need to remember that God helps those who help themselves, and put forth the required effort to achieve the success that is our birthright.

Satan deludes us with earthly illusions of worldly success and attainment, which spring from our ignorance of Eternal Truth and Reality, and we come to fear loss of material possessions, disease, pain, accidents, and death. In our soul, in oneness with God, He has already granted us all that we truly need. In our soul, we already know all we need to know.

The greatest way to bring back the remembrance of divinity is through meditation. Meditation helps us to experience our soul, where we know that, like Jesus, we are a Christ. Meditation opens us up to the divine treasures within. For example, when we go inside ourselves we begin to unfold the soul quality of intuition. God does not need to reason. He knows everything by pure intuition, and so can we by becoming one with the Infinite Intelligence, or Christ Consciousness.

When we go deep in meditation we realize we are the soul, beyond all limitations of the body and the world. In that realization we can remain centered in the calm of the soul and be even-minded in every situation.

God created everything as the creative expression of good. God also created Satan from the same original blueprint of good and beauty. Satan, however, has misused his free will and independence to go against God's perfect plan. Since God has given everyone the precious gift of freedom and independence, He will not withdraw His gift of free will, even from Satan. God did not intend suffering when He created the world and mankind, but in order to give us freedom of choice, the possibility that we would misuse it and create suffering was unavoidable.

Satan is destroying God's perfect plan by tempting humans so that they will think and act selfishly, unwisely, and without love and thus bring in the destructive elements of disease, harmful bacteria, warfare, and so on. However, since God is the originator of thought and all of creation is manifested by materializing the ideas of God, Satan could not manifest and use the destructive elements unless God had created the potential for this in the first place. Since God has thought of everything that could possibly happen, Satan could not think of anything that has not already been thought of by God. For Satan to think of and manifest something that God had not already thought of is impossible.

The relativities and contrasts in creation are God's original ideas to create a cosmic show. Without them there would be no entertainment or show at all. Everything humans needed in order to live in happiness and manifest good and beauty was given to them in the Garden of Eden, but Satan tempted them with the fruit of "the tree of the knowledge of good and evil" and they took his advice. As a result, the perception of evil and good as dualities–counterfeit knowledge–canceled out spiritual knowledge and replaced it. This is the reason for God's warning to Adam, "You may freely eat of every tree of the garden [sense of the body]; but of the tree of the knowledge of good and evil [in the midst of the garden] you shall not eat, for in the day that you eat of it you shall die."

Satan and evil entities try to get us to accept debilitating and destructive thoughts and impulses, such as hate, jealousy, fear, greed, suspicion, half-truths, and selfishness, so that we will act on these thoughts and impulses. God and divine beings try to get us to accept thoughts and feelings that are strengthening and constructive, such as loving kindness, courage, sharing, trust, and honesty, so that we will act on these thoughts and feelings.

Satan's power is limited mainly to influencing humans to do wrong but humans must also take responsibility for the negative state of affairs in the world, as they accepted Satan's influence to do wrong. Also, in the beginning, they misused their free will by judging and condemning pain, even though it was far less intense at that time and served a good purpose. Such judgments caused them to lose their consciousness of the oneness of everything and, instead, to perceive dualities and separation from God.

Unfortunately Satan has made many aspects of physical creation a nightmare and tries to keep us reincarnating here, thinking we can find total fulfillment and perfection on the earth plane. Fortunately everyone will finally figure out that nothing in this physical realm can satisfy our hearts and that only God can do this.

When you feel tempted to be less than your Christ-Self call on Jesus. Jesus struggled and was victorious over every temptation that Satan placed in his path. Jesus became a Christ by his own self-effort in overcoming Satan's subtle tests. So, along with meditation and sincere self-effort, remember Jesus can uplift us. Jesus knows, better than we do, the games Satan plays in his attempts to limit us, and if we follow his guidance, he can lead us back to our diamond essence. Jesus is constantly working to help us realize the truth in his declaration: "Ye are gods."

The Grace of Love

Our saving grace is the internalizing, or attractive, force of love, the Christ Consciousness, who continues to create everything in beauty and harmony according to God's original, perfect plan. The internalizing force of love is stronger than the externalizing, delusive force of Satan, and eventually everyone will once again realize their oneness with God.

To manifest our diamond essence and to realize our oneness with God we need to cooperate with the internalizing force of love and manifest positive qualities in our life. We also need to employ righteous activity to manifest good in the world.

Jesus walked on earth knowing his oneness with God. He was able to dance in the play of creation and its oppositional states without losing his awareness of the One Sole Reality. That is what God expects of each one of his children. Jesus knew how to lift the veil and perceive unity and is trying to help us do the same. Satan wants us to keep the veil intact, preventing us from seeing the Changeless Reality or Truth. God has given us independence and the free will to choose between Christ and Satan.

So here we are in the "game of love," and our perfect diamond consciousness is in a body, immersed in the contrasts of the world. We are swimming in a sea of duality, with opposites swirling around and within us: good and evil, joy and sorrow, peace and restlessness, life and death.

As already mentioned, it is God who is responsible for creating our magnificent souls and the beauty of the world. The Lord is responsible for creating variety in unity, but is not responsible for creating evil. This was due to Satan's tempting of the first humans (Adam and Eve) in the Garden of Eden and their taking the bait. And Satan is working on keeping us stuck, suggesting in our minds that we identify with negative rather than positive aspects of human nature by choosing vengeance instead of forgiveness, over-indulgence instead of moderation, and so on.

By means of evolutionary promptings from within our souls and experiences in the world, God is helping His diamond-soul children to evolve to higher states of wisdom and consciousness. Through the yearning in our hearts, and our free will to choose between what leads to blissful happiness in God and what keeps the soul in the misery of ignorance of God and bondage to matter, we eventually choose the positive attributes of self-control, love, gratitude, forgiveness, peace and joy and renounce greed, selfishness, judgment, condemnation, jealousy, anger and hate.

Eventually we realize that our perceptions of duality, such as seeing good and evil as opposites and apart from each other, are veils that separate us from our divine nature and therefore from God, the Sole Reality. In deepest meditation we go beyond all oppositional states and realize that our diamond-soul essence has always been–and always will be–one with the One Creative Source just behind the dream of creation.

God created everything, including us and Satan, from the power of His loving thoughts and thus made possible all the happenings in the cosmos. He, therefore, is in part responsible for our misfortunes. Although we are responsible for our choices, it is God who created Satan, and the *potential* for us to be subjected to temptation and the painful consequences of our mistakes. Thus the Lord is partly responsible for the mud we have placed on our diamond essence. But remember, the mud resulting from our wrong choices and actions is not our true reality at all and, no matter how long it takes, we ultimately will be liberated from delusion and return to the paradise of union with Him.

Since God made evil possible by thinking of it, and Satan is tempting us to manifest it, tell God He is responsible for the idea of evil and the resulting troubles you and the world find yourself in and that you need His assistance to help you behold your brilliance once again.

God has given us free will and the freedom to choose from any of the many courses of action available to us. If you did not have God's gift of free will you would be like an android (a robotic machine) and thus would be but a victim of circumstance, of cause and effect, and would have little of the divine essence within you. Since God has given us free will we can be co-creators with Him. If we place mud on our diamond nature (by wrong choices) and distort the perfect image of God within us, our diamond essence is nevertheless still there, only hidden.

Since God has given us the power of reason and intuition, He expects us to uncover and realize our diamond soul essence, our Christ-like nature, and then, as His immortal children on earth, shine His light and love on all. When we rediscover our lost heritage we will awaken to

63

our infinite potential and beauty, falling in love with the true diamond essence we and others are.

If we accept that God existed alone before creation then we can also accept that the only substance God could create us with was Himself. God did not create the universe out of nothing. God is everything, and if a void existed, God would have been that, too.

If God created humans in His image and likeness, then Jesus' proclamation that we are "gods" is literally true. We are a ray or portion of God. When the soul is encased in lower forms it is not aware of its divine essence but when it evolves to the human level and does the work to liberate itself it knows, as Jesus did, that it is love and light, forever one with God, and that separation from God was only a dream.

We cannot be lost forever. God has created us in His perfect image and has placed in our soul the quality of love. We may be tempted by the lure of material possessions and passions and may be under these influences for a long period of time, but eventually we will begin to remember our soul essence and yearn to, once again, be consciously at one with God. Then we will be able to reclaim and re-establish our eternal covenant with God and manifest our true state of being.

God knew, in creating us, that if we fell we would not be lost forever and that, in time, we would become disillusioned with the ways of the world and begin to remember Him. As this happens and we get glimpses of divine beauty and begin to experience the sweetness of divine love, we yearn for more. Eventually this yearning pulls on our consciousness and draws us toward unity with the Christ Consciousness, helping us to realize it is God alone who can totally fulfill and satisfy us.

I mentioned earlier, but it never hurts to emphasize it, that unfortunately nearly everyone misinterprets the soul's inner yearning and longing for happiness as yearning for things of the world. Since we experience duality instead of God due to the fall of the first humans, our awareness is outward on matter. God has placed us in Creation and recognition of our soul's perfection is hidden, so we first experience and develop cravings for material possessions and sensory experiences.

Delusion, being extremely captivating, continually tries to convince the mind to believe that, if we just had this material thing or that sensory experience, life would be just grand. Temporal things, however, can never truly satisfy us, but due to the influence of delusion we continually chase after them in our pursuit of happiness. Eventually after so much suffering and misfortune, we finally get the message and realize that things of the world can never satisfy our deep inner longing and thereby make us truly happy, but will always leave us with a feeling of being unfulfilled.

God has created this show of creation to entertain us, but at the same time, has made the different aspects of creation changeable and ephemeral, so they will never fulfill us. The secret is that only God can totally satisfy our hearts.

Since we are initially caught in the play of duality it is inevitable we are going to make mistakes, sometimes major ones, and God realizes this. God's original intention was for us to have a perfect existence, to view contrasting experiences as entertainment only and not get mixed up with the cosmic show, but the misguided, destructive force, or Satan, is working to destroy God's perfect plan of goodness and beauty.

God understands it is going to take time for us to rise above Satan's influence and our material attachments, and to realize our perfect soul nature and act as immortal children on earth. God sent Jesus and other avatars (fully Self-realized beings who come to earth as saviors of mankind) to help us and show us the way. Jesus liberated himself and is always encouraging and uplifting us to do the same.

God, being unconditional love, does not judge us. It is the law of cause and effect, which God has activated in the universe to keep it in balance and harmony that does the judging. Since God has given us the gifts of reason to discern and freedom to choose, if we do make a negative decision and go against God's universal laws we will reap the appropriate consequences. God, in loving tenderness, however, is constantly aware of our perfect Christ-like nature no matter how many mistakes we have made. If we make mistakes, even major ones, God's loving compassion is ever ready to forgive us. God, however, expects us to learn from our mistakes and do better next time. If we have buried our eternal Self under a lot of mud and cannot see our holiness, God is always guiding and supporting us, helping us to remove the mud so that we may once more see that we are made in His perfect image.

To say we are sinners is to be caught up in the realm of delusion. The greatest sin is to consider oneself to be a sinner. We are the immortal soul and this is the reason for our covenant with God and His promise.

Everyone is a Christ in the making. Yes, by God's command we have been immersed in a sea of experiences that we perceive in terms of good and evil, and we may temporally make mistakes (which God anticipates as we are learning in the school of life) and soil our Diamond Self, but this slavery can only be a temporary state of existence. We should not identify with our mistakes, since we are immortal children of God, but learn from them. Often the passage in Romans "For all have sinned and come short of the glory of God" has been blown out of proportion to somehow indicate we were created as sinners and born defective. We were created by God in His blessed image as a perfect, not a defective, manifestation of His creativity.

Romans also states: "The wages of sin is death." This simply means death to the awareness of our diamond essence, our pure, Christ-like nature. Our soul can never be lost or die, but it can be temporarily hidden from our awareness in slavery to the senses. When we do the appropriate inner work our true nature will be revealed, our soul consciousness will be reborn.

If we make mistakes it does not mean we must die and spend an eternity in a place of eternal suffering. A God of unconditional love could never, and has never, created a realm to inflict an eternity of suffering on someone who has made a mistake in this world of relativity and delusion. To believe a loving Lord of compassion could create such a dimension is error.

The hell the Bible is referring to is to be identified with a limited human body and mortal consciousness, unable to feel divine love or happiness, consumed in the burning fires of negative thoughts and unquenchable earthly desires and living in hellish circumstances as a karmic consequence of wrong thoughts and actions. Until such time as they have a change of heart and mind, would this not describe the state of consciousness and actual experience of many people while they are here on earth and in lower regions of the astral world after death?

If we break God's laws that govern physical, mental, and spiritual well-being, we will have to pay the price until we learn to live in love, forgive, and change our ways, as we have gone against the guidance of our higher nature and God, and become less aware of our pure diamond essence. If we are suffering due to our wrong choices, especially if this tendency has become a chronic habit, we will have to make a greater effort to overcome this tendency and purify ourselves. In other words, we may have to use the strong detergent of self-control to cleanse the mud from our diamond essence.

God is omnipresent in the sense that His consciousness embraces, and He is aware of, all things. He knows of human suffering and waits for us to change.

God gave us the gift of eternal life when He created us as perfect, immortal souls. Since God has placed our pure, taintless soul in a mortal body we are both human and divine, just as Jesus was.

The immortal part of our consciousness is our perfect soul, our Christ-like essence. Philip tells us in his Gnostic Gospel that "a horse brings forth a horse, and a man begets a man, but God brings forth a god." The soul that lives in the mortal body comes forth from God.

Our human element is consciousness identified with the limited physical body and mortal mind, engrossed in perceptions and thoughts of the material world. In spiritual teachings, this part of us is called the ego. It is because the ego is attached to things of the world that moral imperfections, or sins, occur. In essence, anything that eclipses our awareness of our divinity can be called a sin.

In his gospel Philip talks about an inner and an outer. He says there is something outside the outer, which the Lord calls "outer darkness" or "destruction." The first outer is the senses and the second is the material world. When the mind is completely occupied with the outer material world of sensations and objects to the exclusion of any inner perception then there is what Jesus referred to as outer darkness and destruction of the spiritual life.

It needs to be remembered, from the quoted passage in Isaiah, that God, as the externalizing force, has created many of the contrasting states that we perceive as dualities: light and darkness, far and near, above and below, for example. And by thinking of every possible occurrence, He has made it possible for Satan and humans to manifest evil as well as good. The play of opposites reigns in the kingdom of the world. If the world is experienced in divine consciousness, these things are not experienced as opposites but as aspects or parts of God as The One. In the kingdom of God there is oneness—a unity transcending all apparent opposites. This is why Jesus encourages us to "make the two into one, the inner as the outer and outer as the inner, above as below." Jesus says in Philip's gospel, "Light and darkness, life and death, right and left are the rule of opposites in life and are inseparable. Those who transcend these opposites are exalted and remember their eternal nature."

Unfortunately, while we are here on planet earth we lose awareness of our immortal essence—our omnipresent soul, or higher self—and spend some time to reclaim our divinity. From my experience of different lives and my intuitive awareness I am convinced God has placed us, His pure immortal children, in creation to enjoy His cosmic dream of creation and at the same time not to forget our oneness in God.

In the Gospel of Thomas, Jesus said to His disciples that when people ask where they come from tell them, "We come from Light, a Light that came into being spontaneously on its own and is manifesting through our image. We are children of the living Father." Jesus then offered solace to his disciples and all true seekers by reminding them they "came from God's kingdom and to this blessed realm they will joyously return."

Jesus' role is to help us identify with our perfect soul essence once again and reclaim our immortal nature as a Christ. Jesus is a perfect example, as he did the necessary work to bring about his own salvation in a previous life. Jesus was victorious, for he overcame his lower nature to realize his perfect Christ nature. Jesus awakened to his divinity, realizing that he was in Christ Consciousness, and is constantly encouraging us to do the same.

Through his unconditional love for God he became one with Spirit and awakened his consciousness to remember all the attributes of Spirit. In his oneness with God Jesus is able to forgive you of your sins—transgressions against the laws of God—and through his grace help uplift you to his state of consciousness if you are attuned to him. When we awaken and behold that we are enlightened souls, we will automatically see that we have always been saved and have but to remember our divine status. However, this requires more than just a belief in Jesus.

Since Jesus accomplished the true purpose of love, realization of his unity with God, and, thus, with all humanity, and knows the way of doing this, he is a perfect model to follow. Your life work is to make yourself receptive to receive his help and grace, to quicken your evolution in God's love and to know that you are indeed a Christ.

Jesus is totally awakened to his Christ stature and he is ever helping you to awaken to the same state of awareness. When you work in harmony with Jesus and realize your oneness with him you will be aware of your immortal soul nature and will be able to reclaim your birthright of salvation and remember your eternal life in God.

In your liberation in Christ you will find final rest from your struggles and at last remember you are whole and complete, deficient in nothing.

In the Gnostic Gospel of Philip, Jesus performs a miracle that vividly demonstrates he can purify and transform us: Jesus went into the dye works of Levi and took seventy-two dyes of different colors and threw them into the vat. The cloths in the vat all emerged as pure white. Jesus then said, "He the Son of Man came as the dyer." If we trust and surrender to Jesus, He can help us awaken to our pure, infinite, divine nature and radiate our essence in the world as white as the snow

Jesus revealed his divine status when he said, "I and my Father are one" and "I am in the Father and the Father in Me." By this he meant that he had united his consciousness with the consciousness of God. Jesus, however, never claimed that he was God or the Only Begotten Son of God. He did proclaim that what he achieved is the destiny of everyone, and, by uniting his consciousness with the consciousness of the Father, he was able to show others how to do the same. If through Jesus' help we uplift our consciousness to and unite it with the consciousness of God as the Son omnipresent in Creation, and then with God as the Father beyond Creation, we too can claim that we are one with God and that we are in the Father and the Father is in us.

By awakening your soul awareness you will be able to uplift and inspire others. Creative manifestations will flow through you to help you uplift humanity and bring them from darkness to the light. When this happens you will be able to manifest Jesus' affirmation in your own life and also say with authority: "Ye are gods."

11

Grace and the Inner Work of Salvation

Many people confess Jesus and accept him as their personal savior. At an historical point in their life, they experienced tremendous inspiration and felt they were converted and born again. As long as they are inspired they feel they have permanently transcended their former negative habits. This encouragement and inspiration may last their entire life if an extremely supportive environment surrounds them.

In many cases this inspiration may be short-lived, and bad habits may come back in double force. This happens because stubborn habits that are initially pushed to the background of the subconscious mind while one is under the influence of a transforming conversion are still in the subconscious mind and begin to present themselves when spiritual enthusiasm wanes. Many people begin to feel they are worse off than they were before their conversion because their negative tendencies are seen in sharp contrast to their born-again consciousness. Saint John of the Cross called this state the Dark Night of the Soul, and many seekers go through this state in their search for union with God.

At this point some people may leave the spiritual path, as it did not afford them the permanent conversion in Jesus they were promised and had hoped for. Their error was in depending solely on *belief* instead of working hand in hand with him to attain a permanent state of consciousness rooted in their savior and his virtues.

The following quote from Ephesians is often used as a justification of the idea that we cannot do anything toward our salvation except believe that Jesus died for our sins and this alone is sufficient: "For by grace are ye saved through faith: and that not of yourselves: it is the gift of God: Not of works, lest any man should boast."

I believe one of the greatest deceptions when interpreting the New Testament is the idea that we only have to believe in Jesus and do not have to do any serious work ourselves for our salvation. Did not Jesus call the Scribes and Pharisees hypocrites for closing the door of heaven against men, preventing them from entering the kingdom of God within themselves, saying: "For ye neither go in yourselves, neither suffer ye them that are entering to go in."

In Philippians there is a passage that advises us to "work out your own salvation." In Corinthians we also read, "Every man's work shall be made manifest: for the day shall declare it, because it shall be revealed by fire; and the fire shall try every man's work of what sort it is." I practice prayer and meditation every day, and I can testify it takes tremendous discipline and "work" to enter within oneself.

It is true God has set up the cosmic plan whereby we cannot achieve the ultimate final emancipation or salvation by our outer work alone. Positive work can give us tremendous good karma and we may reap incredible rewards through our external service. For salvation, however, we are required to do *inner* work to prepare our consciousness to fully receive Jesus and our Christ-like nature.

Jesus has declared the only way to achieve the ultimate salvation is to follow the first commandment to love the Lord with all one's heart, soul, mind and strength. This requires great inner strength or work, as normally we give our love exclusively to the world and many rarely think of God at all. For many, a Sunday service is the only uplifting time in a life of almost total forgetfulness.

When a person first begins their relationship with God and Jesus, they may have many uplifting experiences and grace to keep them motivated. They feel the inspiration of having a love relationship and romance with Jesus. They feel the excitement of being connected with the Lord and the numerous blessings they receive. Very often they begin to focus on what they can get from God and focus their spirituality on what material things they can attract to themselves through God's help. Of course, this is important, but if we want to go deeper in our relationship with Jesus we come to a point where we become more focused on what we can give him rather than what we can receive, and this is a deeper expression of our love for God.

Jesus gave his entire life to God. It is interesting to note that Jesus did not have a house and expensive things yet most of his disciples today live a moderate lifestyle, expecting the best of material goods, and are disappointed when they are deprived of them. Jesus was a renunciant and willingly gave up many material possessions in his search for God.

Hidden away in a Tibetan monastery there are priceless records proving that Jesus lived in India, Nepal and Tibet during his seventeen lost years, from thirteen to thirty, which are not accounted for in the Bible. The records speak of a Saint Issa (translation of "Jesus") from Israel "in whom was manifest the soul of the universe." Nicholas Notovich, who published the book *The Unknown Life of Christ*, tells us that he saw and recorded material from ancient manuscripts preserved in the Himis monastery outside Leh, which were an account of Issa's (Jesus') years in India, Nepal and Tibet. Swami Abhedananda also saw the manuscripts in the same monastery, which supports the information in Notovich's book. Nicholas Roerich, renowned artist, explorer and archaeologist, saw similar records and heard various tales of Issa (Jesus) throughout the East. "Isa," which means Lord, was another name given to Jesus in the East.

From these records of his early life, we know that Jesus gave up worldly things in his search for God-realization.

Sometimes God will purposely take material things away from us if we are attached to them and our attachment presents a flaw in our love for Him. God loves us unconditionally and wants us to love Him unconditionally under all circumstances and not only for His gifts.

In time we will learn to love God simply for Himself and not just as appreciation for satisfying our own needs or the forgiveness of sins. Through direct experience of God a lover of God comes to love the Giver more than His gifts (material possessions and forgiveness) and desires to give their whole life to God and merge in God's infinite love and light.

Saint John of the Cross tells us that *those who truly love God are content with nothing less than God.* They are then more interested in giving their love to God than receiving God's material gifts. This is maturity in our relationship with our Creator and is manifesting our love for God in a higher way.

When we give our love completely to God, we open ourselves up to the ultimate experience of blissful oneness with God as love, light and omnipresent consciousness and know our Christ-like essence.

To make sure we learn this vital lesson to deepen our love for God there will come a time in the life of every disciple of Jesus when God and Jesus will take away these perks (experiences) and will say, "Now that you have felt my blessings and support, you must do the necessary inner work. You show Me you are serious about your love for Me and your salvation."

You must *prove to God by your spiritual efforts that you want Him more than anything else.* When you have proven your love by doing the sufficient inner work of loving God more than anything He might give you, then God will lift you up and unite you with His state of consciousness and your salvation is assured. The final union with God can only come through God's grace; it does not come by mere works or belief alone. But you do have to show God that your love is unconditional. God watches the heart to see if you will purify your love so you love Him for what He is and not for what you can receive from Him.

In Thomas' Gnostic Gospel Jesus confirms this and tells us how to enter the kingdom of God. When he saw infants being suckled he told his disciples: "Those who enter the kingdom are like these infants being suckled." These children were pure and innocent, in perfect, loving surrender and trust in the presence of a nurturing mother. Jesus indicates we need to approach God in the same way.

God cannot make you love Him. Genuine love is unconditional, freely-given, and your love needs to be unconditional, a free gift of your heart. This is the love that God and Jesus have for you, and this love is what they seek from you.

Paul promised us in Romans: "And we know that all things work together for good to them that love God, to them who are called according to his purpose." When we love God in this manner then we can truly love our neighbor as ourselves and be a true Christ.

12

Jesus' Mission and Supreme Sacrifice

Jesus was called the Christ but this was not the name given to him at birth. It was a title signifying the anointed of God or chosen by God. Jesus had attained Christ Consciousness and therefore was a master. Anyone who attains the Christ Consciousness state by dissolving their ego in the Infinite Consciousness may also be called a Christ. Jesus performed the holy work of realizing his true Self, not as the body or personality of Jesus the "Son of man," but as the vast ocean of Spirit, "the Son of God." As a fully realized master, one with God, Jesus can help uplift you to the same state of consciousness that he has, and at God's behest, he is helping all those who look to him for guidance, to overcome the world and attain salvation, just as he did.

When a great soul like Jesus comes on earth they have a special mission to reveal divine truth to the world, uplift humanity and liberate advanced disciples. Jesus was an avatar, having been fully liberated in a previous incarnation, so God entrusted him with a multipurpose mission.

Jesus was fully aware of the purpose of his life and what he needed to accomplish. Jesus came to show the love aspect of God and total trust and faith in Him. Jesus also came to teach the religious leaders the spirit of the law. He emphasized that even if they were following the Torah, or Law of Moses, their hearts were far from God. Jesus mission was to help mankind attain the same level of consciousness he attained. Jesus *especially* came to show the way to become a Christ and one with God

74

by entering within oneself, and taught His disciples how to do this. Jesus often proclaimed, "The kingdom of God is within you."

Jesus knew if he confronted the spiritual leaders, even though it was for their benefit, he was putting himself at risk. Jesus also knew the history of his country and how the religious leaders persecuted and even killed so many of their own prophets over the centuries. Jesus fully understood if he challenged the religious leaders of his time he would open himself up to the same fate as that of the former prophets. Indeed, this is exactly what happened.

Jesus was struck down at the height of his career and in the prime of his life; he was only 33. But in a supreme act of love he willingly sacrificed his body, demonstrating the majesty and power of complete surrender to God, for which he prayed in his immortal words: "Thy Will Be Done." Jesus knew the Will of God was for him to demonstrate the immortality and omnipotence of the soul, and this is why Jesus said, "Destroy this temple, and in three days I will raise it up."

Jesus understood the Law of Karma God has put in operation in the Cosmos (to every action there is always a reaction, or we reap what we sow) so he willingly sacrificed himself to nullify the past bad karma of others. He had little or no bad karma of his own, but took on that of others in letting himself be crucified. He had the spiritual power to prevent this, but he willingly surrendered to the authorities, suffering greatly, and in his resurrection showed he had power over death. His life, death and resurrection have inspired countless souls down through the ages.

Former prophets were able to foretell of Jesus' mission and predict his ultimate death and sacrifice. They could detect the karma of the Jewish nation and accurately predict the probable outcome.

Jesus' death on the cross was not prearranged by God but was a gift of love from Jesus in which he purposely suffered in his own body the karmic consequences of the actions of others. One should understand that God does not reward or punish anyone. God has created a universal spiritual law, or mechanism, by which one receives like compensation for the good or evil they have created by their thoughts and actions.

While on the cross Jesus lovingly worked in harmony with this law by taking the sins of his disciples and others upon himself to best pay off their debt. By this pure act of love Jesus freed his disciples from the karma of their past limiting actions to make them qualified to receive the Holy Ghost, or Comforter, and become Christs.

Was Jesus' sacrifice on the cross supposed to take away all the sins of the world? If it did then the world would have improved dramatically after his death but unfortunately history tells us that humankind's consciousness became darker. The Romans in Jesus' time were more civilized than those of later generations, who watched with glee people being killed in most horrendous ways as entertainment in the arenas.

Five hundred years after Jesus' life was the darkest period for humankind so Jesus' death on the cross did not redeem the future sins of the world. But this period would have been even darker had he not come to earth to help us.

Jesus' hands are tied if we merely believe in him for salvation. Jesus is all-powerful but he can do nothing if we do not co-operate with him and do the inner work ourselves. To think that we are born sinners and are totally corrupt and can do nothing for ourselves in our salvation is a copout and a subconscious desire and excuse to not make the effort. Jesus supports our efforts with his grace and transforming light as we work in harmony with him. Jesus warned us not to say "Lord, Lord, Lord," and not do the things he tells us to do. Jesus clearly said to go within ourselves, for "salvation is within" us.

Jesus' death on the cross activated many positive consequences for the world at large. Jesus was aware of the tremendous impact his sacrifice would have for generations to come. There are so many lessons we can learn from his passion.

Jesus' nature is absolute tenderness. He portrayed this in his final hours and showed the superiority of tenderness over brute force.

Jesus had all the power of the universe at his command and could have wiped out his aggressors with one act of his will, but he did not do this. This shows his tremendous strength and self-control.

Who is able to truly forgive anyone who has wronged them? Forgiveness is indeed a noble quality of the highest degree. Jesus exemplified forgiveness even to the point of forgiving those who were crucifying him. Praying for those who were putting an end to his mortal body he said: "Father, forgive them for they know not what they do."

Jesus loved all with a universal love, not only friends. He rejected no one, accepting and loving even those who considered themselves his enemies.

Jesus' mission of love manifested right to the last breath of his mortal body. It is an ongoing mission, which continues to this day. Jesus proved in his life he was indeed a Christ. As a reward Jesus is ever one with Universal Unconditional Love and blesses those who make themselves receptive to his infinite compassion.

Jesus' death on the cross shows us how truly great he is, as he manifested flawlessly his divine virtues. Jesus' death gives us hope and inspiration that we too can overcome our imperfections and realize our sinless, immortal soul, as he did.

Philip mentions Jesus' death on the cross several times in his Gospel. He says the apostles called "the power of the cross" "the right and the left." Through the power of the cross along with one's own effort Christ unifies all dualities and "a person is transformed and no longer is a Christian but *becomes a Christ.*"

Jesus was very advanced in spiritual progress so he was able to handle the cross. This was part of Jesus' mission but not necessarily ours. I remember counseling a very dedicated woman who gave up her meditation practice and became lukewarm in her spiritual life. After digging deep in self-exploration we found she had a hidden fear that in order to prove her love for God and be a true disciple of Jesus she would have to go through tremendous suffering and perhaps experience a physical cross herself.

This subconscious fear set up a barrier between her and Jesus. Jesus had a special role to play and had to deal with the authorities of his day, and death on the cross was the unfortunate consequence. Jesus is not asking us to suffer unnecessarily. We need to keep our body and mind in good condition so we can meditate properly as Jesus did in the Garden of Gethsemane.

We do need, however, to bear our daily cross with the right attitude regarding all situations or difficulties that come to us of themselves. Let us all be so in love with God that no external cross can touch us and diminish the awareness of God's love and joy that we feel inside.

Through the "power of the cross" and our efforts to be in tune with Jesus' Christ Consciousness we will be able to experience the underlying unity in all things, including good and evil, pleasure and pain, and all other dualities, and know our true nature as love, light and immortal consciousness—a perfect reflection or image of the glory of God.

In Jesus' passion, he felt for others and could sincerely say, "Father, forgive them for they know not what they do." Jesus' compassion for others while on the cross had transforming power. Jesus could feel the outer pain of the nails in his hands and feet, and the hate, viciousness and evil directed toward him, but except for the interval when he uttered the words, "My God, my God, why hast thou forsaken me?" he was fully aware of his oneness with God and the power and glory of God that dwelt within him. Firmly rooted in his eternal God Self during the three days after his death on the cross, he resurrected his body, and during the next forty days, he frequently appeared to his disciples and many others in his spiritualized, resurrected form, talking with them, inspiring and uplifting them, and then vanishing before their eyes. By the example of his life, death, and resurrection Jesus is a guiding light for the world.

Above all, Jesus fully manifested the first commandment to love God with all one's heart, soul, mind and strength. Jesus demonstrated his supreme love for God and his god-like nature in all his actions.

If we accept Jesus as our personal savior, it is our privilege to endeavor to exemplify every one of his virtues. Jesus overcame all limiting temptations, and we have the opportunity to walk in the footsteps of our perfect model and become a Christ, just as he has done. Jesus constantly encourages us to renounce the idea that we are sinners, and to live and act like "gods." If you want Jesus to save you, commune with Him in the inner silence and receive him in your soul, so that you may become a Son of God, a Christ.

Jesus is the Guiding Light for us to follow. If we attune ourselves with his transforming Light and allow it to shine through us, we will also be able to become beacon lights in the world. By being a perfect mirror of the Light of Christ we will have the blessed opportunity to help others see the divine Christ Light in themselves.

13

Jesus, the Perfect Model

Purify yourself by accepting Jesus Christ into your life so he can be your helpmate and assist you in transforming your life. By using your free will and accepting Jesus as your personal savior and above all keeping your thoughts in tune with his and following his teachings and counsel, lamb-like, Jesus can help you purify yourself through his grace and uplift you to your true Christ-like stature.

When you were created, God, as the Creator, made you as an eternal expression of divine Light and Love. As God's child, you have an eternal relationship with God and need but to remember what you really are. You were and still are, in essence, a perfect, immortal soul, possessing divine, creative power and free to accept or reject the love that unites you with God. Jesus can help you remember the love that you are and that God has for you. Belief in Jesus (or another enlightened being) is the first step; in order to purify yourself completely you need to become conscious of the transforming Light and Love of God.

When Jesus died on the cross he showed the world an incredible example of his divinity. He also received and canceled the past bad karma of his disciples and others, purifying and uplifting his disciples so they would be ready to receive the Comforter, or Holy Ghost. When they received the Comforter they became established in their divinity and were then fit to preach the gospel to the world.

Jesus also will forgive bad karma in our time and lead us to salvation if we do our share of the necessary work to purify ourselves and make ourselves receptive to receive his grace. We need to become true disciples of Christ and do the preliminary work, just as his first apostles did.

Belief in Jesus and accepting the idea he shed his blood for our sins and granted us salvation is not enough.

Also, believing that we are not required to do any work on our part, using as a justification the quote from Ephesians, "For by grace are ye saved through faith and that not of yourselves; it is the gift of God: Not of works, lest any man should boast." is self-defeating. It is true that the final merging in God comes solely from God's grace, so Paul is correct, but we need to do a tremendous amount of work to purify our consciousness to receive that grace. Using the excuse that we are just sinners does not get us off the hook but is simply a subconscious desire to avoid making a definite commitment to follow Christ one hundred percent and do the necessary work he requires.

If you believe you should receive a new car, do you just sit and wait for it to come? No; you put in the necessary effort to acquire it. Why, then, expect salvation to come effortlessly just because you believe in Jesus and belong to a church.

Salvation is a personal matter between each soul and God. You have to individually make love to God. Jesus will encourage you to make love to God; he cannot do it for you. Church membership may be helpful in fostering an inward relationship with God but is no guarantee of an inward relationship and is not a substitute for it.

Saint Ignatius wisely said that he did not have time for God's grace so he met Him halfway using his will.

We have free will to choose. The power that is in us is our own, but it is God-given and God expects us to use it. Neither God nor Jesus will use it for us. Jesus cannot change our thoughts and actions; only we can do this. Through an initial belief in Jesus we may feel his presence of grace and mercy. We may feel a tremendous transformation in our life and feel we are born again.

To realize we are a divine soul and become re-established in our diamond essence we need to establish our *oneness* with Jesus; we need to bring Christ fully into our consciousness. We are required to do the inner work so we may become attuned to His state of consciousness and become a Christ.

Jesus promised that everything he manifested we can manifest as well if we do it in his name. This means being consciously connected with him and being a perfect channel of his virtues. Since Jesus is one with Spirit and manifests all the attributes of God, being at one with him will help us realize our own divinity as well.

From St John: "Verily, verily, I say unto you, he that believeth in me, the works that I do shall he do also; and greater works than these shall he do."

Remember, Jesus fasted, meditated and prayed in order to realize his oneness with God and was then able to manifest the presence of God in His service to others. He practiced inner discipline not just to set an example for humanity but because it enabled him to be in constant communion with God and manifest his divine soul essence.

In Mark we read, "Very early in the morning, while it was still dark, Jesus got up, and left the house and went off to a solitary place where he prayed. Jesus often spent time alone re-establishing his union with God. Matthew tells us, "And when he had sent the multitudes away, he went up into a mountain apart to pray; and when the evening was come, he was there alone." Jesus often spent the whole evening in prayer and meditation.

In his life on earth Jesus was fully human but knew his divinity. Like all of us he had lived before in a human body; and in a previous life, after many lifetimes of striving to perfect and awaken himself, he came to realize the universal, Only Begotten Son state of consciousness, or Christ Consciousness, within himself and became a Christ.

Jesus is a Son of God but not the only Son of God. John reminds us that as many as received Him (Christ Consciousness) to them gave He the power to become Sons and Daughters of God.

Many claim that God has only one Begotten Son: Jesus. They then say it is only when we accept Jesus into our life that we become an adopted son or daughter of God and have been brought into the family of God. But in essence we are all immortal children of God (not adopted) just as much as Jesus, and we simply need to experience this, to live in full awareness of our immortal essence, as Jesus did.

It is true that God has only one Begotten Son, or Daughter, who is the Christ Consciousness (beyond gender). The nature of the *Only* Begotten Son of God, or "Christ Consciousness," is a universal state of consciousness that permeates all of creation. Jesus uplifted his consciousness to become one with Christ Consciousness and remembered he was a true Son of God.

Many Gnostic Christians from the first two centuries AD express in their writings an understanding that the "Only Begotten Son" is a universal, cosmic principle (consciousness or intelligence) in Creation rather than the person of Jesus. I explain this state of consciousness (Christ Consciousness, or Only Begotten Son) that Jesus attained–and is possible for you to attain–in much greater detail in my books *Conversations with Christ* and *Meditation: Where East and West Meet.*

God has manifested a pure reflection of His Supreme Intelligence, or Wisdom, out of Himself as His Only Begotten manifestation, Son (or Daughter), to create and maintain the world. The only begotten Son (or Daughter) is the intelligence residing in the first manifested vibration (Light or Holy Spirit) emanating from God as the ever-existing, Supreme Spirit beyond cosmic vibration.

Any soul who uplifts their consciousness to vibrate in resonance with this sacred, refined vibration (the Light of God) and beholds the Heavenly Father/Divine Mother through it will be saved. In the Gnostic Gospel of Philip he tells us we cannot only "put on the perfect light but can become the perfect light."

Jesus accomplished this in his life and uplifted his consciousness to become one with the Only Begotten Son state of consciousness, and by doing so fully realized his Christ-like nature. In other words, Jesus fully received the Light of God and the Universal Christ Intelligence within the Light and became awakened to his immortal nature as a Son of God. Jesus then lifted his consciousness through meditation to even greater heights, where he realized his oneness with Spirit beyond cosmic vibration. What Jesus accomplished is the destiny of each and every one of us. We also can accomplish what he accomplished, through his help, or grace.

Jesus never claimed he was God or the "Only Begotten Son of God." It was the Church, at the Council of Nicaea (AD 325) and later at the Council of Constantinople (AD 381), that proclaimed Jesus was the only Begotten Son of God and also God. The Nicene Creed states: "the only begotten Son of God, begotten from the Father before all ages, light from light, true God from true God, begotten not made, of one substance with the Father."

This creed is correct in its description of the universal Only Begotten Son as "light from light, true God from true God, begotten not made, of one substance with the Father." Jesus *attuned* himself to and became one with the love, light and intelligence of the Christ Consciousness—the consciousness of God omnipresent in Creation. The distinction should be made that Jesus was not the only human being to become a Christ by uniting with the Only Begotten Son, or Christ Consciousness; Krishna and other avatars have done the same. In this remembrance, or union, Jesus became one with the consciousness of God omnipresent in Creation. We are all children of God and can do exactly what Jesus has done and remember that we too are one with the Only Begotten Son (or Daughter) of God. This limiting Nicene Creed was made law and had enormous implications for Christians, Jews, and later the Muslim community. It also has caused untold confusion in claiming that Jesus is the *only* Begotten Son, leading to many religious wars and the Inquisition.

Jesus' only claim was that he was one with God and the Only Begotten Son, and this is a state of consciousness that everyone can eventually attain. As the wave can become one with the ocean so the soul can realize its oneness with God, but the soul can never claim it *is* God. The wave cannot claim it is the ocean, even though it has become one with it. Along with Jesus we can claim we are a Christ, one with God, when we become Self-realized, but we can never claim that we are God.

Jesus clearly stated the Father was greater than he and he also said: "Why call me good when there is none good but one and that is God." Jesus clearly dedicated His life to uniting himself with God and doing God's will.

Jesus, if he were God, would never have asked the Father why he had forsaken him during his passion. Jesus, if he is God, cannot forsake himself. Jesus truly felt a separation from his Heavenly Father on the cross and he expressed it.

The Gnostic Gospel of Philip refers to Mark's passage when Jesus said on the cross, "My God, My God, Oh My Lord why have you forsaken me?" Philip indicates that Jesus temporarily "left that place" of divine consciousness–the Christ Consciousness state in the holy of holies (the bridal chamber).

Also, if Jesus was God, why did he need to pray? Prayer is communion with God; if he was God, he did not need a special time and place to commune with himself. No, Jesus was spending his evenings communing with God and re-establishing his unity with Him.

Jesus clearly said, and encourages us, that we can do all that he has done and more. This is why Jesus is such a tremendous inspiration for all of us: he was a mortal just like us and awakened to his divine immortal nature.

Jesus, in the lifetime as we know him, became fully Self-realized, re-established in his sinless soul essence. He had accomplished this transformation in a previous lifetime, but even enlightened souls are influenced by earthly consciousness if they are reborn in a physical body. On earth one experiences the world by means of the physical senses and thinks in terms of concepts drawn from sense experience. Earthly consciousness veils direct experience of the greater reality behind this world, and a great master who returns to earth in a physical body has to overcome this influence and reestablish full realization of God. Jesus achieved this and more. After his physical death on the cross, Jesus resurrected his body and ascended in Spirit. Thus, he fulfilled his prophecy to resurrect his body in three days.

Jesus exemplified total fulfillment of the Law of Moses by perfectly following the Ten Commandments in his life. Jesus also fulfilled and transcended the Law of Moses through his single-pointed faith, and devotion to the Heavenly Father and humanity. He fully resurrected his soul into Omnipresent Spirit, and his selfless, redeeming act of love on the cross combined with his resurrection blesses all humanity and was the final victory. Being fully established in the kingdom of God, Jesus was able to demonstrate the power and glory of God and is a savior, or messiah, for the world.

Jesus can be an example for us because he was tempted just as we are, and he overcame temptation and found victory over every obstacle. He is an inspiration to us because he did the inner work of purification and was victorious. He has set the blueprint for us to follow, and by attuning ourselves with him in our thoughts he will guide us to be victorious in our own lives. Jesus through his own example showed us how to become a Christ.

As I have already stated, Jesus spent his evenings in meditation and prayer. Why? Because he was re-establishing his complete oneness with the Heavenly Father so he could say with authority: "I and My Father are one" and claim to be a Son of God. Jesus' mission, if you accept him as your personal savior, is to uplift you so you too can become awakened and say, "I and my Father are one; I am a child of God." You may prefer to claim, "I and my Mother are one; I am a daughter of God."

There is no way Jesus can help you achieve conscious oneness with God unless you try to follow his example. He entered within himself in meditation in the garden of Gethsemane, and the Bible tells us in many other locations as well, such as in the wilderness and on the Mount of Olives. He could claim with authority, "The kingdom of God is within you" because he found it within himself. He knew the kingdom of God was not of this world because he transcended this world of duality and found the New Jerusalem within himself. He was fully established in the Love and Bliss of God and taught his disciples to experience this as well. The disciples received and became firmly established in these states when Christ sent the Comforter to awaken them.

Jesus' message to all of us could be stated thus: If you love me (my Christ Consciousness) and keep my commandments you shall receive the Comforter—invisible, cosmic, intelligent, vibratory power, or energy, (word) that sustains the universe.

If you yearn to be a disciple of Jesus, it is necessary to tune in with him by doing the inner spiritual work, just as he did. In the Gospel of Thomas, Jesus says: "The solitary and elect [those who enter the silence within themselves] are blessed, for they will find the kingdom of God."

Meditation Modeled by Jesus and the Mystics

Meditation is the key that helped Jesus and other God-realized souls to become awakened to the infinite potential within them. They learned to commune with God and experience Him in the inner silence and stillness of their soul. Psalms reminds us to be still and know God. In that stillness the meditator can know the soul as one with God by expanding their consciousness from material consciousness to God consciousness. The soul has only one way to go; it must go back to God through efforts in meditation and devotion to God.

In meditation it is ideal if one can straighten the spine ("make straight the way of the Lord") to facilitate seeing the light and hearing the sound of the Holy Spirit (baptism through the fire of cosmic energy).

A straight spine is a tremendous aid, as then one's life energy more easily flows inward and up the spine enabling one to receive the higher states of consciousness. If one has physical challenges then one is advised to do their best and allow God to withdraw the energy into the higher chakras in the spine through His grace. It is important to realize that a personal relationship with God and one of His representatives, such as Jesus, and offering one's devotion to God and His representative are more important than techniques or bodily discipline.

The illumined mystic Saint John of the Cross relates his own experiences of God as the Holy Ghost in Stanzas 14 and 15 of his classic, *Spiritual Canticle*. He describes the "roaring torrents" as "a spiritual sound and voice overpowering other sounds and voices in the world...." "This voice, or this murmuring sound of the waters, is an overflowing so abundant as to fill the soul with good, and a power so mighty seizing upon it as to seem not only the sound of many waters, but a most loud roaring of thunder." But the voice is a spiritual voice, unattended by material sounds or the pain and torment of them, but rather with majesty, power, might, delight, and glory: it is, as it were, a voice, an infinite interior sound which endows the soul with power and might. The Apostles heard in Spirit this voice when the Holy Spirit descended upon them in the sound 'as of a mighty wind,' as we read in the Acts of the Apostles."

When someone asked Jesus why there are so few that are saved, Jesus reply was, "Strive to enter in at the strait gate: for many, I say unto you, will seek to enter in, and shall not be able." The strait gate is meditation and Jesus very well knew that few would be able to enter within themselves except his disciples and close followers. The kingdom of God was reserved for them because Jesus taught them how to meditate and go within. The masses were unfortunately not receptive to this advanced teaching of Jesus and were mostly interested in his miracles.

In the Gospel of Mary Magdalene Jesus appears to his disciples and greets them saying, "Peace be unto you." Jesus then encourages his disciples to receive his peace unto themselves. He warns them not to be led astray by others who say look here or there for the Son of Man. He emphasizes that the Son of Man is "within you and if you seek Him diligently and earnestly within yourself you will surely find Him."

Saint Teresa of Avila encourages the nuns in her charge to go within: "If you want to find God, my sisters, you have got to seek Him inside. He is within you." Saint Teresa says the inner path to God begins with belief and adoration (which can include praise) but ends in Spiritual Marriage, or oneness with God.

With these beautiful words, Saint John of the Cross encourages us to meditate and go within: "What more do you want, O Soul! And what else do you search for outside, when within yourself you possess your riches, delights, satisfactions, fullness and kingdom—your Beloved [Jesus] whom you desire and seek? Be joyful and gladdened in your interior recollection with Him, for you have Him so close to you. Desire Him there, adore Him there. Do not go in pursuit of Him outside yourself. You will only become distracted and wearied thereby, and you shall not find Him, nor enjoy Him more securely, not sooner, nor more intimately than by seeking Him within you."

In loving God with all their strength, the consciousness of these saints shifted from sensory distractions, outward emotions, and identification with the body toward realization of and identification with the soul. Through their intense devotion, their divine, life energy was interiorized and rose upward within them, awakening spiritual centers in the spine and brain, and they discovered the exalted state of "mystical marriage," where their soul merged with God and became one with Him. Some were able to pass their consciousness through the "single eye" in the forehead and merge into Christ Consciousness. And some speak of going breathless and finding their soul soaring to spiritual heights. They truly loved God with all their heart, soul, mind, and strength.

In the Gospel of Thomas, Jesus' advice is to "fast with regard to the world" if we "want to enter the kingdom of God." Jesus also says, "We need to observe the Sabbath as a real Sabbath" if we "would see our Heavenly Father." The true Sabbath is not only a rest from worldly preoccupations, both physical and mental, but the deeper esoteric meaning is to enter into the eternal silence within ourselves by fasting from our intellect, memory and imagination, closing the door to all these faculties and truly resting in the intuition of the soul.

If our desire is to be one with Spirit–to be in tune with the ultimate state of consciousness–we should know that this state of awareness is beyond all vibrations, or motion. It is only in perfect stillness that one rises above all motion to achieve oneness with the One Changeless Absolute. Once that final union is achieved on a permanent basis, then one is a fully-enlightened master and is able to live in that perfect awareness of union with God no matter what they may be doing, even performing intense physical activity performed to please God.

When we are calm we can behold the beautiful, loving face of our Eternal Blessed Mother and Father. However, the indescribable beauty of the Blissful Infinite usually can be beheld only in perfect stillness. Once perfect stillness is achieved then one may advance to the state of being in union with God all the time.

Model Jesus and make meditation and prayer a daily ritual you practice faithfully. As you create the necessary *stillness* you will experience your diamond nature once again and the mud of limitations will be released from your life.

Jesus will lift you upon his bosom of omnipresent, unconditional love as you practice this. You will realize you are never alone but have always been and ever will be endowed with a divine consciousness. Remember, your awakening is Jesus' commission from God and he will unfailingly work with you until you are liberated in him and become a Christ, at one with all beings and all Creation.

14

Why Should You Seek and Dedicate Your Life to Jesus?

For Joy

Jesus is the fullness of joy, or bliss. Those who have felt his presence in prayer and meditation testify his joy is greater than anything the world can possibly offer. My personal experience is that Jesus' joy is beyond description; no words can suffice.

You will eventually come to the point in your life where you will realize it is only this kind of joy that can totally satisfy you. Jesus' joy is sufficient; it is complete.

For Wisdom and Guidance

In Christ's joy you will feel his indwelling wisdom and support guiding your life.

God has created everything out of Himself. Since the universe is His cosmic body, He knows all there is to know. There is nothing He does not know.

Jesus in His oneness with God is omniscient. When you are in tune with Jesus you will inherit some of his supreme wisdom and he will flawlessly guide your life. If you intend to sincerely serve him, then even if you make a poor judgment or mistake he will help correct the error.

Jesus knows you better than you know yourself and through his unfailing wisdom and guidance he is ever trying to help you evolve to your highest potential.

For Love and Understanding

Jesus is a pure channel of the love of God and his love is ever available for you. Jesus' love for you is unconditional. Others may give you their affection for a period of time and maybe forsake you, but Jesus will never forsake you.

The pure love of Jesus is the only love that can satisfy your heart. When you love Jesus you are loving love itself, and his love can never disappoint you.

Even if the whole world seems to turn against you and misunderstands your motives, Jesus understands you and is ever offering his unconditional loyalty and support.

For Healing

Jesus continues his healing ministry in the world. If you have the required faith and trust in him, Jesus can heal you of your physical, mental and emotional disharmonies. There have been saints, however, who went through tremendous suffering and did not receive physical healing, but Jesus worked at a subtler spiritual level and liberated them. St. Francis bore the wounds of Christ and suffered greatly, but still no amount of pain or discomfort could take away the unconditional love he felt for God. This is a deeper aspect of spirituality.

Eventually the body wears out and one dies. Jesus healed Lazarus when he brought him back from the dead, but like everyone else, at some point Lazarus had to leave the body behind. So it is important to remember that, just as he eventually did for Lazarus, on a soul level Jesus can help you remove the disease of ignorance that is separating you from experiencing your ever-pure Christ nature.

For Experiencing the Necessary Power for Success

God is the source of all the power of the cosmos, and this infinite power flows through Jesus' consciousness at all times.

When you tune in with his consciousness you will begin to realize your consciousness is not limited to a mortal body and its experiences, but that you are immortal. With Jesus' help all the chains of limitations will be broken, and when you concentrate on an endeavor that is in harmony with the Will of God, his power will flow through you to help you achieve material, mental and spiritual success.

For Overcoming Fear

You have Jesus' infinite power to support you. When you realize you can accomplish all things through him, fear will no longer be able to resonate in your being.

As you tune in with Jesus and remember you are an immortal being, nothing will be able to make you afraid. The realization unfolds that nothing can limit your consciousness and that, as eternal consciousness, you will never cease to exist.

For Security and Protection

This world is a play of duality and is ever changeable and can never offer you a haven of security and protection. Jesus' nature is changeless peace, love and joy, and being constant, only this divine, eternal consciousness can give you the security and stability you need.

For World Unity and Peace

The Christ Consciousness within Jesus is omnipresent and is within all people and all living beings. When we can feel this divine presence, this loving consciousness within ourselves, only then we can truly love ourselves, knowing our soul is a spark of God.

When we can feel Jesus in others and know they too are a child of God, we can love everyone with Christ Love, a love that is impartial and pure.

When we become one with Christ and realize we are omnipresent and are in everything and everything is within us, then we truly can love the whole world as ourselves. We then become a true peacemaker in the world, loving everyone equally. It is then that we fully express our Christ potential.

If everyone strived to accomplish this, heaven would be established on earth.

For Freedom from Limiting Habits

The healing Light of Jesus can cauterize all the limiting circuits in your brain and help rewire you to manifest his positive virtues. In Christ's Light, disharmonies and disease cannot exist. Your job and joy is to make yourself receptive to receive Jesus' transforming Light.

For Fulfillment of All Desires

To commune with Jesus is more satisfying than the fulfillment of any worldly desire. All other desires pale in comparison when one has attained the inner perception of Jesus' indwelling presence.

Jesus has promised us that, if we first seek the kingdom of God, all things will be added unto us. Through the testimonial of my own life I know this is true. When we dedicate our life to knowing Him and doing His will, God automatically fulfills our lesser desires.

An Overview

The purpose of life is to know God, and we can be united with Him through Jesus. By continually seeking Jesus and learning to give him our unconditional love, our spirit will be uplifted. In divine love and trust, there is only the joyous, eternal assurance of God, and we will discover an inner realm where there is no pain, disharmony or striving. In time, we will be able to remain in this realm while we are living and working in the world. We will then have become fully established in our Christ-like essence as an immortal child of God.

In order to love Jesus with all your heart, soul, mind and strength you require a concept of Jesus you can really love. I invite you to consider the attributes of Jesus listed in the next chapter.

15

Receiving and Serving Jesus

How can you behold Jesus and receive his presence? You can nurture your relationship with Jesus in many different ways. You may approach him in an intimate personal way as your Father, Mother, or Child, as your Friend or Elder Brother, or as your Beloved. Since Jesus is one with God you can feel his presence as pure Spirit. Jesus will come to you in whatever way you hold most dear and precious.

Jesus is right within you and he can be perceived by hearing his voice or feeling his beloved presence. These perceptions of Jesus are an intuitive experience.

Let us start with the *feeling* aspect of receiving Jesus' presence. If we allow ourselves to be receptive, we can open our hearts to Jesus' essence of unconditional love, and through his infinite compassion and mercy we will be able to feel his undying love for us. In appreciation, we can offer our love for him in return. The more we love someone, the greater is our trust in the person. The same is true in our relationship with Jesus.

Faith in Jesus helps us to know him. When we have total faith in Jesus and surrender to his will he will take charge of our life and move us in the direction of our highest growth and fulfillment. Jesus will lead us down whatever path leads to oneness with him and the Heavenly Father.

Jesus' nature is pure peace. As Jesus was able to calm a storm, he can quiet the turbulence of our restless minds and still the static of fear and worry in our hearts.

The deeper we rest in Jesus' being, the more we will be able to experience him as absolute bliss and feel a state of rapture and ecstasy that will totally nurture and sustain our soul. Christians today are taught to focus on an event sometime in the future deemed appropriate by God, when they will experience a state of ecstatic rapture. The truth is, the state of blissful rapture is already a part of our inner diamond nature; only this state is presently hidden from us. When we can interiorize our consciousness and feel Jesus' blissful nature, we will be reunited with our own bliss consciousness. It is then that we will have received the true rapture promised in the Gospels.

Jesus' vibration is very subtle and refined. He is supremely sensitive, calm and tender. As you learn to uplift and refine your own vibration he will embrace you and lift you even higher so that you may resonate in harmony with his gentle nature. In resonance and oneness with Jesus you will realize that every virtue Jesus has is your divine birthright as well. When you are united with Jesus he will be able to awaken you to your divine remembrance as a Christ.

Jesus exemplified complete humility in everything he did or said. He is exalted because he was a perfect example of humility. Jesus is ever ready to humbly serve you in your evolution back to God and help you manifest true humility in your life.

Through misinterpretation of the Bible some people see and approach Jesus as a judge, tyrant or taskmaster. This is not Jesus' role nor will it ever be. You are his own and you can make him your own by trusting and surrendering to his ongoing and supportive love for you. Jesus yearns to reveal himself to you.

Jesus is omniscient, or all knowing. In his oneness with Spirit there is nothing he is not aware of. Through his faultless intuitive perception he knows what is happening simultaneously in every aspect of creation. He is aware of the number of hairs on your head and not a sparrow falls outside the blessed sight of Jesus. Call on him in times of trouble, as he is able to offer you his unfailing wisdom and guidance.

Jesus also knows us better than we know ourselves and what is best for us. If we give him our life and ask for his assistance he is ever available to uplift and transform us into his likeness and image. When we are in resonance with Jesus we will be able to manifest his virtues in our daily life and truly manifest our Christ-like nature.

The consciousness of Jesus is omnipotent; he contains all the power of the universe. You can access his power and strength to help you accomplish all the positive things you want to manifest in your life. Through attunement with him you can feel his consciousness coursing through your nerves and body, filling you with his strength.

The Gospel of Philip tells us that, to those who are devoted to him, Jesus usually appears not as he truly is, but in the capacity that they are able to receive. "To the great he appears as great, to the small as small, to the angels as an angel and to men as a man. Due to this, his Word [infinite, omnipresent, omnipotent nature] is usually hidden from everyone." Saint Teresa calls this hidden, sublime nature of Jesus *the formless Christ*.

Although such a blessing is rare, Philip declares that on the Mount of Olives Jesus appeared to his disciples in his glory and transformed them so they were not only able to see Jesus in his glory but become one with him in his glory. Beholding his work manifested in his disciples, who through his grace had merged their consciousness in the perfect Light of the Holy Spirit, Jesus, in gratitude, asked them to "unite the angels with them also."

Jesus yearns to help us see him and become one with him in his glory, but in order for him to give us this grace, it is necessary for us to do the work and become receptive to him, as his disciples did.

Jesus as Spirit is pure, undiluted Cosmic Light. Through his body of Light he is spread evenly throughout the cosmos. Trillions upon trillions of galaxies are swirling in Jesus' Cosmic Body. In the Gnostic Gospel of Thomas, Jesus eloquently talks about his omnipresent, omniscient nature as the Christ Consciousness residing in all things: "Split a piece of wood and lift a stone and you will find me there." Jesus proclaims that he is in everyone, and everyone comes from and extends from his Christ nature. Jesus yearns that we become one with his omnipresent consciousness. Our liberation demands that we return to the omnipresent consciousness that lives in Jesus and all fully-liberated souls.

The perception of Jesus' Light, which is the Light of Christ Consciousness, can be seen in the spiritual eye, the single eye Jesus refers to in the scriptures. "The light of the body is the eye; therefore when thine eye is single, thy whole body shall be full of light" (Luke

95

11:34). After one first begins to see this Holy Light in deep meditation, one can, by continued deep meditation, merge in it and experience one's omnipresence as the immortal Self, and ultimately expand in it throughout eternity.

In the New Testament when Jesus asks others to drink of his blood he does not mean his physical blood, but the blood of his Cosmic Body running through the veins of the universe, nourishing every cell and atom in Creation. When Jesus says blood he is referring to the omnipresent Light of his Cosmic Body. When he uttered these precious words, Jesus obviously was not asking those who were with him to drink of the physical blood of his mortal body. Jesus taught this truth in his ministry before his Last Supper. Therefore, at the Last Supper, when Jesus said, "Drink my blood in remembrance of me which is shed for the remission of sins," his disciples already understood Jesus was speaking to them in symbolic terms and was referring to his Cosmic Energy, or the Light of his omnipresent body.

At the Last Supper, Jesus' disciples were aware of the symbolic meaning of "drink my blood" because Jesus had previously taught them to meditate, to go within and experience his consciousness as "Light." We know Jesus revealed hidden truth to his disciples because he told them, "it is given unto you to know the mysteries of the kingdom of heaven, but to them it is not given."

Jesus had already asked the Jews not only to drink his blood but to eat his flesh (meditate and experience him as the Cosmos and the Cosmic Light running through it) long before the Last Supper. In John we read:

"The Jews then murmured at him, because he said, I am the bread which came down from heaven.... Verily, verily, I say unto you, He that believeth on me hath everlasting life. I am that bread of life. Your fathers did eat manna in the wilderness, and are dead. This is the bread which cometh down from heaven, that a man may eat thereof, and not die. I am the living bread which came down from heaven: if any man eat of this bread, he shall live for ever: and the bread that I will give is my flesh, which I will give for the life of the world. The Jews therefore strove among themselves, saying, How can this man give us his flesh to eat? Then Jesus said unto them, Verily, verily, I say unto you, Except ye eat the flesh of the Son of man, and drink his blood, ye have no life in you. Whoso eateth my flesh, and drinketh my blood, hath eternal life; and I will raise him up at the last day. For my flesh is meat indeed, and my blood is drink indeed. He that eateth my flesh, and drinketh my blood, dwelleth in me, and I in him. As the living Father hath sent me, and I live by the Father: so he that eateth me, even he shall live by me. This is that bread which came down from heaven: not as your fathers did eat manna, and are dead: he that eateth of this bread shall live forever" (John 6:41, 47-58).

The Jews and also many of his disciples did not grasp the deeper metaphysical meaning that Jesus was trying to covey to them. Jesus was trying to use terms that the Jews could relate to, as they had received Manna (bread) from God when they were in the desert. Only a few of them would have understood what he meant if he had said "inner light or energy" so he had to use terms that most of them could relate to. Many of Jesus' disciples by not understanding the deeper meaning of his words and the gift he was offering them walked away.

"Many therefore of his disciples, when they had heard this, said, This is an hard saying; who can hear it? When Jesus knew in himself that his disciples murmured at it, he said unto them, Doth this offend you? What and if ye shall see the Son of man ascend up where he was before? It is the spirit that quickeneth; the flesh profiteth nothing: the words that I speak unto you, they are spirit, and they are life. But there are some of you that believe not. For Jesus knew from the beginning who they were that believed not, and who should betray him. And he said, Therefore said I unto you, that no man can come unto me, except it were given unto him of my Father. From that time many of his disciples went back, and walked no more with him. Then said Jesus unto the twelve, Will ye also go away? Then Simon Peter answered him, Lord, to whom shall we go? thou hast the words of eternal life. And we believe and are sure that thou art that Christ, the Son of the living God" (John 6:60-69).

Jesus' close disciples came to understand that Jesus' words "flesh" and "blood" referred to his state of consciousness (Christ Consciousness) and not his physical body. It is because they experienced Jesus' consciousness in their own expanded consciousness that they knew "eateth my flesh" and "drinketh my blood" means merging their consciousness into the Christ Consciousness by partaking of the sound and light of the Holy

Ghost vibration. Some of the Gnostics came to understand this deeper truth of Jesus that was handed down by the apostles to those who were receptive.

Jesus continues to ask all his disciples around the world to enter within themselves and drink deep of his "light" that they may expand with it and eventually become one with him in his omnipresent "formless" body.

By being one with Jesus' Cosmic Light (blood) we are raised beyond our mistakes (sins) and become established in our sinless, immortal nature. This is what Jesus meant by the remission of sins.

These original Christian views were later replaced by the official church dogma of transubstantiation. This doctrine states that the bread and wine used in the Eucharistic rites are mystically transformed into the physical body and blood of Jesus when blessed by an ordained priest during the liturgy of Holy Mass.

When the Gnostics celebrated the Eucharist they would have known it symbolized the experience of partaking of the spiritual "flesh" and "blood" of Jesus. Philip understood this truth and in his Gnostic Gospel said, "Jesus' flesh is the Word and his blood is the Holy Spirit." Many of Christ's disciples and early Christians "ate" and "drank" from his Omnipresent Consciousness in the all-pervading sound (word) and light of the Holy Spirit and therefore understood his true meaning.

The Light of Jesus contains all-sufficient healing power. When awakened in the receptive devotee, the healing Light of Christ can cauterize negative seed tendencies lodged in the brain and spine. When these limiting thought patterns and resulting disharmonious energy patterns are removed in the Light of our blessed Lord Jesus Christ, many of a disciple's sins are washed away and the disciple is purified.

Jesus' intention was to send his Light to his disciples and purify them when they would receive the Comforter (Holy Sound and Light) at Pentecost.

Jesus' blood is the Cosmic Light and his body is the Creative Sound. Within the Light and Sound is the intelligence of the Christ Consciousness, which guides them as they manifest God's will throughout the cosmos. Jesus' Light vibration has a refined sound indicating its activity in creation. This Holy Sound has been called by many names in the Bible: Holy Ghost, Comforter, Trumpet, and Sound of Many Waters. At Pentecost Jesus came to his disciples in his Cosmic Body of Light and Sound as the Holy Ghost vibration. The disciples heard him as a "sound from heaven as of a rushing mighty wind" and saw him as "cloven tongues like as of fire and it sat upon each of them."

The Holy Spirit is an aspect of God as a threefold being: Father, Son and Holy Spirit. Nevertheless, God is one and is the Supreme Consciousness in which all things are one. By stilling the restless mind and through pure love and devotion, you can receive and experience the Sound and Light of the Holy Spirit just as Jesus' disciples did.

If you would receive Jesus' Cosmic Light and Sound Vibration you need to develop stillness in order to make your consciousness an empty vessel so he can dwell in you and take up all the room. Jesus' Light and Sound can only be perceived by the faculty of intuition, as they are too refined to be perceived by the ordinary senses. Listen within at the center of your consciousness and you will hear his Holy Voice whispering to you his eternal words of Changeless Love.

The intelligence inherent in Jesus' Cosmic Light (Blood) and Cosmic Sound (Word or Body) is a loving intelligence and is called the universal Christ Consciousness or Christ Intelligence. When Jesus' disciples received Jesus' Cosmic Vibratory Light they were filled with this Divine Intelligence, or Christ Consciousness, the true Only Begotten Son.

By blessing his disciples with his cosmic essence of Light, Sound, and Christ Consciousness, Jesus was able to awaken them and bring all things to their remembrance. Thus they were able to spread the gospel with newfound wisdom and boldness. When the disciples spoke, everyone was in awe, as they heard the message in their own language.

In the same way, Jesus will reveal his divine Christ Consciousness to you. Jesus will comfort you with his all-redeeming intelligence (a pure reflection of God's Supreme Intelligence) and bring all things to your remembrance when you make yourself receptive to his awakening and transforming universal presence.

It is a spiritual necessity to make ourselves receptive to receive the Light of Christ and its inherent Cosmic Sound and Christ Intelligence so Jesus will then be able to bathe us in this subtle and refined healing Light and awaken our diamond Christ-essence once again. My books *Conversations with Christ* and *Meditation: Where East and West Meet*

offer detailed instructions on how we can receive the Light of Christ
with His Cosmic Voice and Christ Intelligence and transform our lives.

The Gospel of Philip offers us a tremendous revelation: "When you
see and know the Spirit you can become the Spirit, when you see and
know the Christ you can become the Christ, and when you see and
know the Heavenly Father you can become the Father." Philip explains
that what a worldly person sees outwardly they do not become. They
may see the sun but they do not become one with the sun. In the inner
world, "in that place," what you see and know you may become.

Jesus as the universal Christ Consciousness, or Only Begotten Son,
is ever within us, every ready to awaken us to our divine, cosmic, loving
Christ nature.

You can receive Jesus by working with him for others. Since Jesus is
one with the Light of God and this Light is coursing through his body
of the universe, Jesus' consciousness resides in each and every atom of
the cosmos and everything is in his love. Jesus' loving consciousness is
within you and in everyone you meet. By serving others, you are truly
receiving and serving Jesus. Remember, the person before you has the
potential to become another Christ. By helping everyone you meet, you
are assisting in the awakening of the Christ potential within them.

If Jesus is your divine preceptor do everything for God and Jesus.
The more you think of Jesus and strive to please him, the greater will
be your receptivity to him and the greater awareness you will have of
his presence.

When you act for yourself it ends there, but when you act for
God and Jesus your acts expand to infinity. These acts will be eternally
present in the heart of Jesus. Since Jesus lives in the eternal now, beyond
the world of relativity with a past and future, everything is ever new for
Jesus. Your noble actions are ever new and fresh in his Consciousness.

Jesus is one with the owner of the cosmos–God. What you do for
Jesus he will offer to God and contribute to God's cosmic plan of love
and good will.

To tune in with Jesus we need not only to call on his name but
also to do his will as recorded in the Gospels. Just as God has created
physical laws of the universe, there are also moral and spiritual laws.
Jesus encourages us to live in harmony with those laws, not only by
following the Ten Commandments but also by loving and serving God

and our fellow human beings. When we do this and when we have developed a certain degree of spiritual realization, then we are fit to preach the Gospels to others. First we need to preach the Gospels by the example of our own lives, and then by vocal expression as well.

The closer we come to Jesus the greater will be our desire to sing from the depths of our heart of the love of Jesus. Our only earthly desire will then be to help uplift others so they too may rest on the lap of Jesus' unconditional love and realize their immortal Christ-like nature.

16

The Bible

The Bible is an inspired book written by many different authors. It contains stories to inspire us and contains a solid foundation for moral living and the way to know God and tune in with His will.

The words of Jesus, in his oneness with God, are the living Word of God. They inspire us and can lift us beyond our normal limited consciousness into the awareness of God within us.

Any of the other intimate conversations with God by God-realized authors or the eternal truths they perceived that are accurately recorded in the Bible are also the sacred word of God. Thus, the Bible is the literal word of God as it is conveyed to us through these sacred passages.

Some of the authors of the Bible, however, did not have complete God realization and may not have had direct communication with God. To have direct communication with God requires deep spiritual advancement and insight. The passages written by these authors may not have been the literal word of God.

That God or His Holy Spirit dictated the Bible to these authors of lesser realization and that the passages they contributed are the inerrant word of God is questionable. Of course God can do all things, but He has given everyone free will and choice. He does not sit a person down and say this is what I want you to write and these passages, someday in the future, will be included in a book called the Bible.

The first written Old Testament was about 300 BC, though it contained historic words from 10 centuries before. Many of the passages of the Bible may have been inspired by God or given to His servants, but it is necessary to consider the human element in writing them down. Due to the human factor there is a possibility of errors and inconsistencies.

If God dictated the Bible to His servants, and God's words were written down right away and passed on to future generations exactly as they were received, the Bible would be faultless, having no errors or inconsistencies. God is omniscient and knows everything. In God there cannot be any contradictions.

Unfortunately, the Bible does contain many contradictions. These inconsistencies can only come from human error, since God is omniscient, and therefore these passages are not the literal word of God, but the words of men.

Consider also that some of the Bible is recorded history and poetry. Moreover, Paul even said that on some issues he did not have the commandment of the Lord and offered his judgment as a faithful servant of God. He goes on to say he *thinks* he has the Spirit of God. In view of this, how could Paul's letters of encouragement and instructions to the churches be considered the direct word of God?

Some of Jesus' teachings were "hard teachings." His disciples did not fully understand everything he said. Also if Peter, who is a direct disciple of Jesus, said Paul's writings contained things that were hard to understand, how can one be sure that some of Paul's words are the literal word of God? The standard Christian understanding is that the Holy Spirit has inspired the entire Bible and is "God breathed." How can we be sure?

It is also necessary to consider that errors may have occurred from different translations. Many of the translations were performed by scholars who may have had powerful intellects but may not have had the depth of spiritual realization to accurately translate many symbolic passages.

Since many of the sayings in the Bible are symbolic in nature, they need to be discerned through the power of intuition, as these gems of truth often cannot be grasped by the limited intellect alone. It is necessary to delve deep into these sacred passages through an intuitive study of the Bible, at the same time working on deepening one's spiritual awareness through prayer and meditation.

The Bible is a sacred book; however, it is often the *interpretation* of biblical passages that may be in doubt. Even if a passage is truly the word of God, it needs to be interpreted properly by a person of God realization who is in attunement both with God and the author of the particular scriptural verse.

A God-realized master is omniscient (all knowing), omnipresent (their consciousness resides in every atom of creation), their intuition is awakened, and they are in a better position to interpret the scriptures.

It is important to keep these principles in mind when considering the formation of the first Christian Bible by the Christian Church, recently discovered manuscripts of early Christian writings, and the scholars who were privileged to interpret them.

There are many preachers and teachers today who do not have God realization and tell people not to question the Bible but to believe blindly in their interpretation of what the passages mean. If you begin to question and have any doubts about their interpretation they try to instill fear and guilt to bring you back to their belief. Unless you do as these teachers say, you are told you are deceived and are in a state of sin for questioning them. They convert your questioning or doubt into a moral issue and, if you do not believe what they say, you are considered morally wrong and require forgiveness. Only a God-realized master who is totally in tune with God and the Christ Consciousness can give you the exact meaning of certain Bible passages as it was intended.

As you progress on the spiritual path cultivate your own intuitive insight, and through an intuitive study of the Bible, you may discern truth on your own. It is helpful to take a statement of truth, no matter the source, and not *believe it blindly* but *prove it* in our own life. I invite you to take this approach with my writings as well.

If you want to be a student of truth it is important to learn how to calm your mind, and in a place of stillness and receptivity place your whole attention on a Bible passage and intuit the truth that arises in your calm, attentive mind and heart. God can then speak directly to you through those passages and guide your life.

Intuition is a gift and an attribute of your soul that you already possess. You do not need to acquire it; you need only to develop it. To be a true student of the scriptures the most important requirement is to develop your own intuitive understanding and feel the truth of what you are studying. Once you attain insight into biblical truth you can apply it in your daily life. The Bible will then truly become the living Word of God for you, assisting you in awakening your Christ-like nature.

I invite you to sit quietly and in the stillness reflect on Jesus' words. What does your intuition reveal to you regarding the words of Jesus, "You are gods"?

Conclusion

Praising God, adoring Jesus' personality, and blind belief in Jesus' name do not lead to salvation. Jesus' message of salvation is that the kingdom of God is at hand and it is within us.

How can anyone be eternally condemned by God if the eternal essence of their soul is pure and the kingdom of God is within them?

Jesus is yearning to help us to interiorize our consciousness and expand with his to the Divine Kingdom of Infinity. Salvation comes from experiencing the truth that we are already saved insofar as our soul essence, made in the perfect image of God, cannot change and still is perfect.

Jesus asks us through the Gospel of Thomas to "Follow me for my yoke is easy, my lordship is gentle and in me you will find your repose." In another passage from Thomas, Jesus inspires us when he says: "Whoever drinks from my mouth [becomes one with the same wisdom I possess] will become just like me." Jesus, as the Christ, promises that he will "become us, and all the spiritual dimensions and treasures that are hidden will be revealed to us."

Embrace God within you and experience Him with loving affection. If you take the time to enter within yourself and love God with all your heart, soul, mind and strength you will be richly rewarded indeed. In Corinthians we read: "But, as it is written, Eye hath not seen, nor ear heard, neither have entered into the heart of man, the things which God hath prepared for them that love Him."

Isaiah states that God will give you hidden treasures and reveal to you the substance and mysteries of secrets. The substance of the secrets is God. And then you will experience the fullness of God and will have the perfect vision of God spoken of by Saint Paul.

By going deeply within yourself you will have accomplished the true purpose of your life—Self-realization—knowing that you are indeed a Christ.

About Alexander Soltys Jones

Alexander Soltys Jones is a graduate of Tyndale University, with the degree of Bachelor of Religious Education, as well as a Spiritual Director of the University of British Columbia's Pacific Jubilee Program with the Vancouver School of Theology.

He has practiced meditation for forty-five years and has taught meditation for thirty years.

He has written seven books, including the bestselling *Seven Mansions of Color, Conversations with Christ, Meditation—Where East and West Meet* and *Awaken The Christ Within You*. His recordings include *Angels of Color and Sound* and *Kali's Dream*.

Learn more about Alexander Jones on his website:

www.alexmeditation.com

Books and Recordings by Alexander Soltys Jones

To obtain any of my books, please contact me through my wetsite:

www.alexmeditation.com

Seven Mansions of Color,
Originally published, 1982, Republished by Cygnet Media Group, 2014

This book offers inspirational and practical methods for the use of color in one's daily life. Learn to use the benefits of color to attract harmony and happiness. Saturate your environment with joyous and positive energy to bring new vigor, health, peace, prosperity and spiritual realization.

Topics include: color in the aura and chakras, healing properties of color, spiritual awareness through color, color meditation, color in your home and wardrobe, etc.

Reviews

"Your CD and book on color have been of great benefit to me and to some of my friends and patients. Your work promotes inner healing as well as cosmic harmony." — R. Irons, MD., Libby, Montana

"Several weeks ago I finished reading your book 'Seven Mansions of Color.' For me it is the 'Bible of Color.' I cannot praise it enough. I think it is the best on color therapy that has been written." — Marie Sieigniano, Homosassa Springs, Florida

Creative Thought Remedies,
Originally published, 1986, Republished by Cygnet Media Group, 2014

Creative Thought Remedies uses the power of thought to create the highest form of healing. It condenses the timeless wisdom of the ages into an easy-to-understand visual form. By studying these affirmations and charts, your energies will be channeled so that you may become successful in all your undertakings.

Topics include: what promotes and what diminishes joyous living, success as a way of life, transforming undesirable habits, relationships, virtues and preparation of one's own personalized thought remedy chart.

Reviews

"The book you have written. *Creative Thought Remedies,* is beautiful. Many times I have found myself seeking comfort from your profound insight and inspirations. There are many, many positive thoughts to assist in turning from the negative. Truly a work of art." — Penny Jacobi, Guelph, Ontario

"Please send me as many copies of *Creative Thought Remedies* as the money enclosed will permit. I think it is an incredible book and would like to share it with those who need its wisdom." — David Bobineam, Woodlawn, Ontario, Canada

"The author has distilled the basic spiritual wisdom of the ages, as well as their own experiences and insights, into a number of "thought flow charts" showing the process of conditioning and transformation of basic life attitudes.

The book provides clear maps for understanding the attitudinal patterns which limit and those which enhance spiritual growth. It provides a useful method and framework for assisting counselors and those working on themselves with such transformational tools as affirmations and flower essence." — Richard Katz (The Flower Essence Society) Nevada City, California

"Alex, thank you for writing such a wonderful book. The teachings I put out—I am a rebirther and yoga teacher—use these principles over and over, so it is good to have a book I can so heartily recommend." — Gita, Toronto, Canada

How Much Did You Love? What Did You Learn?
Originally published, 1994, Republished by Cygnet Media Group, 2014

This practical self-help book is packed with affirmations and guided visualizations to help you on your journey to self-actualization. It is based on two questions: How much do you love yourself, others and your Creator? and What are you learning this lifetime to help you live in love, peace and joy?

Conversations With Christ,
Originally published, 2004, Republished by Cygnet Media Group, 2014

Join Alexander Soltys Jones as he shares with you his intimate conversations with Christ and the tender and loving messages he received. Find comfort and support in these inspirational messages from Jesus.

This life-transforming book also contains all the meditation techniques you need for your own personal communion with Jesus and quest for Christ Realization.

Reviews

"I feel that this book gives one the opportunity to share in an intimate relationship with Christ in themselves and it also provides many different meditations connecting them to their Real Self. It is one of the best books I have ever read and I am moved deeply by the author's willingness to share this universal message with everyone. " — Sheron Richards, Bridgenorth, Ontario.

Meditation – Where East and West Meet
Published by Cygnet Media Group, 2014

Author and long time meditation expert Alexander Soltys Jones details a unique approach to the art of meditation that will enrich your life and transform you. Awaken to the divine potentials within you and experience peace, vitality, intuition, love, joy and the presence of God through the practice of meditation.

Awaken The Christ Within You
Published by Cygnet Media Group, 2014

This book will open your eyes to new vistas of spiritual truth, for it shows us that Jesus was referring to the divine power, love and intelligence within our souls—the Christ within us—when he proclaimed, "Ye are gods" and it also reveals hidden truths in many of his other statements.

Christian Meditation
Published by Cygnet Media Group, 2014

Discover and practice methods of meditation that the Desert Fathers, Pope Gregory, Saint Francis, Saint Teresa of Avila, Saint John of the Cross and others used to attain holy rest in God.

Audio Recordings (Music)

To obtain any of my audio recordings, please contact me through my wetsite:

www.alexmeditation.com

Kali's Dream

Joyful piano melodies ripple like cool mountain streams with mood-changing colors like the seasons. Pure and crystal-clear solo piano compositions evoke subtle and beautiful feelings within. The notes express the creative playfulness and depth of Nature in a way that touches the peace and beauty with each listener.

Reviews

"Kali's Dream is so pretty you can close your eyes for your own dream." — OP Music Magazine

"Your music is so beautiful that I will have it played over KAZU. Thanks again for the magical music." — Mike Schmitz (KAZU fm) Pacific Grove, California

"I have your CD Kali's Dream and count it among the most beautiful music I've heard." — Therese Coupz, San Francisco, California

Forever

Here is a unique and spiritualized instrumental recording featuring the guitar, piano and synthesizer. This CD is both peaceful as well as uplifting, a rare combination to find.

Reviews

"I love your new CD. It is very beautiful and inspiring. You seem to be able to translate angels singing onto your recordings." — Joyce Vissell (Author, *The Shared Heart*)

"Inspired by his long and deep involvement on a spiritual path, prolific composer Canadian Alexander Soltys Jones has released this slightly more up-tempo instrumental album. Similar to his now classic *Kali's Dream*, this album is co-created with David White performing all electronic and acoustic instruments. Incredibly moving and expressively gentle. In an effort to communicate his visions in meditation, Alexander creates melodies from the heart. I'd call this 'heightened awareness composing'. Not only does this music bring peace of mind but also deep bodily relaxation even with passive listening ... *Forever* also provides excellent inspirational and motivational music for creative endeavors, as well as housework and driving!" — Renee Gulpi (Music Editor, *Common Ground Magazine*)

Audio Recordings – Guided Meditations

To obtain any of my guided meditations, please contact me through my wetsite:

www.alexmeditation.com

Peace Beyond Stress

Here is a powerful relaxation recording to soothe away the stress and tension of your body and of your mind. Learn how to relax and overcome stress using the most effective and simple techniques.

Meditation 1 gives you time for yourself and encourages you to create a mental holiday on a deserted topical island where all is peaceful and serene. In this place of tranquility, Alexander will guide you to practice the dynamic technique of progressive tension-and-relaxation exercises. They will soothe your muscles and harmonize your body so that you can feel peace reclaiming your life as stress and tensions melt away.

Meditation 2 is a relaxation exercise for the mind. Use this visualization when the mind is restless, thoughts and emotions seem to be racing everywhere, and you feel the need to bring them under control. With a steady mind and heart Alexander will help you focus your full attention on a goal that is important to you until success is achieved.

The music which accompanies the meditations has been specifically created to enhance their beneficial effects. Relax and live the life you want to live.

Reviews

"I have just received your new CD Peace Beyond Stress. After listening to it I am searching for the 'good words' to say how much I appreciate it! The music, singing birds, sound of the sea waves, and your voice so full of 'Great Love' brings a direction in ways to relax." — Isabelle Ryback, Montreal

Angels of Color & Sound

Alex's soothing voice will guide you to balance and awaken your chakra centers through the gifts of the angels. The seven color angels will present you with the treasures of the color rays emanating from the seven chakras: vitality, courage, joy, love, peace, intuition, and soul realization. The background music has been carefully chosen and played in the key note of the chakra to assist you to resonate with each chakra and feel the guidance of the divine qualities within.

Reviews

"My students and I have found the recording extremely constructive for the induced states of relaxation and meditation." — Y. McKinley (Toronto Yoga Center)

"When I hear Angels of Color & Sound I am transported to a healing dimension. The meditation and music are deeply touching and even now as I think of them I feel the rich blessing they impart." — Allen Cohen (Author, *The Dragon Doesn't Live Here Anymore*)